W9-AGP-772

The Art of Accompaniment

MAKING CONDIMENTS

Jeffree Sapp Brooks

1988

NORTH POINT PRESS

San Francisco

Copyright © 1988 by Jeffree Sapp Brooks

Printed in the United States of America

Library of Congress Catalogue Card Number: 88-61176

ISBN: 0-8647-346-3

Illustrations copyright © Chris Muller

FOR NANA

Contents

Acknowledgments

It would be nearly impossible to thank all the dozens of people who in some way assisted me with this book. There are several whose help was invaluable.

First and most important, I must thank my entire family for their staunch belief in me. Specifically, I thank my mother, for endless hours of typing and testing recipes; my husband, Joel, who supported me and this project even though he would rather I had written a cookbook on steak and potatoes; and my sister, Jordana, for listening when everyone else was sick of hearing about condiments.

To the following individuals who contributed their outstanding recipes, I am deeply indebted: Irene Muzio, of San Mateo; Alma Hecht, of San Francisco; Lucille Mayo, of Santa Rosa, and her niece Charlotte Brown, of Oakland; Mary Sargent, owner of the Alta Vista in San Diego; Kimala and Roger Martin, owners of La Brasserie in Oakland; Jeanne Phillips, of the Phillips Farm in Lodi, California; Philip and Nancy Chu, owners of Nan Yang in Oakland; and Tanya Berry of Port Royal, Kentucky.

Still more helped in numerous other ways. Dr. George York of the University of California at Davis answered dozens of questions regarding proper food preservation. Dorothy Wall, of Berkeley, helped immeasurably with the proposal. My agent, Susan Lescher, persisted because she knew (even when I didn't) that this book would get published by the right publisher, and she was right. I couldn't have invented a finer staff of people to work with than the extraordinary group at North Point Press. In particular, I salute Jack Shoemaker and Kate Moses for making this more fun than work.

Preface

Many years ago, when I left the comfort of my parents' house and ventured out on my own, I found little time at the end of the day in which to cook and even less energy to devote to the effort. Yet I refused to give up the great pleasures that cooking provided. I needed shortcuts.

I could, at seven or eight o'clock in the evening, manage something as simple as a broiled chicken breast, a fillet of poached fish, or a mélange of vegetables. Before long I began adding simple sauces, dressings, spice mixtures, and anything else I could think of to enhance the flavor of my quick dinner efforts; I began to rely on condiments instead of time and effort. After a while, condiments became more than a shortcut. Whenever I had free time on weekends I prepared chutneys, flavored butters, and pestos to have on hand during the week. Cooking within time limits became a whole new challenge. Condiments evolved into a way of cooking and eating well.

This book is not only a collection of recipes, but a resource guide and the result of my experimentation with food in that period and all the years since. It is about innovation, taking simple ingredients and playing with them: using an unusual method of preparation, such as making carrots into marmalade or cherries into ketchup; or accentuating what is already familiar in a food, such as turning yogurt into a tart and creamy cheese. While I do not give menus per se, I offer serving suggestions and ideas, such as topping fresh steamed asparagus with Tangerine *Maltaise* Sauce, smothering a bowl of sun-ripened peaches with *Cassis* Cream, or siding slices of Thanksgiving turkey with Cranberry Chutney with Tart Green Apple. Condiments in this sense become intrinsic aspects of the meal, giving dishes that are otherwise ordinary tantalizing new dimensions and variations.

I have always been fascinated with food, cooking, and why

people eat what they do. Some of my earliest memories are of Buba, my paternal grandmother, and her kind, half-moon-shaped eyes. Often she visited us and made strudel from scratch. When she carefully rolled out the soft dough, it gently hung over the sides of our ten-person, pine-wood dining table without so much as a hairline tear. I could look right through it, as though it were chiffon. She spooned the filling along one edge and slowly rolled up the strudel to the other end of the table—without a drop of filling leaking from either end. I remember being terribly impressed and thinking I'd never be able to make strudel. I'm still impressed, and I still can't make strudel.

Food was taken very seriously in our house; it wasn't something to be wasted but was to be enjoyed and appreciated. Mama experimented wildly in the kitchen. In winter she made multiple versions of beef jerky and, in the warmer months, pickles. In my youngest years, I remember the refrigerator being packed during the summer and fall months with fresh pickled cucumbers in quart jars. Later we owned two huge refrigerators that sat side by side. One held regular staples, such as milk, juice, and cheese; the other—year-round pickles. Our neighbors, the Crabtrees, used to laugh at us for being the only family on the block to have an entire refrigerator just for pickles. They also used to eat more of them than anyone else we knew. I hope this book has the same effect on your enjoyment of condiments that Mama's refrigerator had on the Crabtrees' joy from pickles.

Jeffree Sapp Brooks

Notes to the Cook

Here are a few things to keep in mind as you prepare these recipes. First, many of them (excluding pickles and chutney) do not require salt, although recipes list it. Since you may prefer your food more or less salty than I do, I leave it to you to vary the salt accordingly.

Notice that, in such ingredients listings as *1 garlic clove minced* or *1 pound apples, cored, peeled, and chopped*, you are to measure first and prepare second. When ingredients are to be prepared first, then measured, the inversion, too, is specified, for example as *1 tablespoon minced lemon zest* or *2 cups chopped tomatoes*.

Several recipes contain a canning symbol: 🔳 This little jar indicates that the recipe may be canned. If you prefer not to can, keep your condiments refrigerated. For those of you with little or no canning experience, see the appendix, A Word About Canning.

Many recipes using fresh tomatoes require you to peel them. The fastest, easiest, and most efficient method of doing this is to drop the tomatoes in a pot of boiling water for 30 seconds to 1 minute, depending on how closely the tomatoes crowd the pot. Strain them immediately in a colander and pull off all peel by hand before they cool. To also seed the tomatoes, halve them on a cutting board and, with your index finger or a small spoon, scoop out the seeds.

Throughout the book you will notice the terms "chop," "dice," and "mince," for successively smaller-size pieces. "Chop" to ½ inch size, "dice" to ¼ inch size, and "mince" to ⅛ inch. I recommend using a large cleaver (available at Asian markets or cooks' supply stores) to achieve the smallest cut.

Unless you are immune to them, fresh chile peppers can burn your skin when you are chopping, dicing, or mincing them. To protect yourself, it is wise to wear rubber gloves while handling the chiles. If you are brave and decide not to use the gloves, be sure not to touch your nose or eyes, because they can become inflamed.

Generally I call for two types of olive oil, pure (or unspecified) and virgin. Occasionally I recommend extra-virgin olive oil. I base these recommendations on how the oil is used in the recipe. If the oil is to be heated or cooked in any manner, there is no point in using high quality, expensive virgin oils; the heat destroys the delicate "virgin" flavors. Pure oil will do. I only require virgin oils in those recipes that do not call for heating, where you will be able to taste the rich olive flavor of the virgin oil.

If you do not have any "runny" honey, as specified in some recipes, you can heat honey that may have crystallized or become a little stiff over a low flame in a small saucepan. As long as you don't refrigerate the given recipe for too long after preparation, the honey structure should remain "runny."

When making vinegars, it is not necessary to fill bottles to the rim, although it creates a much more attractive effect. For vinegar making, I suggest using glass milk bottles because they hold an even quart and the bottle necks are wide, so you can stuff fruit and herbs in them. I realize milk bottles are not as easy to come by as they once were, but with a little searching (at small dairies, gourmet cookware shops, and antique stores), you can find them. Wide corks work best for sealing them. If you decide not to use the milk bottles or other quart containers, but opt to make your vinegars in smaller bottles, be sure to distribute sprigs or seasonings evenly, so each gets an equal amount of flavoring.

If you don't own heavy saucepans and skillets, I don't advocate you go out and spend a fortune to buy them, because they can cost several hundred dollars. But if you are considering buying new cookware, I do suggest you buy good quality, heavy pans. They will evenly heat the food and make the cooking process easier on you by preventing under- and overcooking. And they will last forever, so the high cost will eventually even out several years down the road.

I also do not urge you to go out and buy all sorts of fancy kitchen appliances. For years I went without a food processor; in fact, I didn't purchase one until 1984. It is possible to cook without one, but a food processor sure does make nearly every kitchen job easier. If you don't own one, you can certainly make the recipes, but bear in mind they will be more time consuming as you prepare ingredients by hand. In some cases, I offer alternatives, such as using a blender, a mixer, or a whisk. There are only a few situations where I recommend the use of a food processor exclusively; in these instances the food processor gave the best results, and since I want you to have those same fine results I offer you the most sensible way of achieving them.

For making preserves, more often than not I suggest using citrus seeds and fruit pits, instead of commercial pectin. These are natural sources of pectin that will jell the preserves during the cooking process. Granted, they do take longer, but in many of the recipes, they create a finer product. Usually I only recommend using commercial pectin in recipes where shortened cooking creates a better result.

Many of the recipes form a froth on the top during cooking. Most cooks skim this froth at the end, just before spooning into sterile canning jars. I think this wastes precious time and brings down the temperature of the preserves, which should be maintained as much as possible. If you skim the froth while it cooks, you conserve the heat and save time.

Throughout this book, you will run across the herb cilantro. Your market may call it fresh coriander or Chinese parsley. Do not confuse it with coriander seeds, which are harvested from the coriander plant and dried.

When a recipe lists mustard seeds, I am asking you to use yellow seeds. Black seeds, often used in commercial mustard recipes, impart a bitterness I do not particularly think suits these recipes.

Bear in mind, there are many ways to prepare jars and bottles for the recipes. Many require strict adherence to canning procedures; these are outlined in the last section, A Word About Canning. But others, particularly those that will be refrigerated, offer a variety of methods, depending on how long the product will keep, if it will be consumed fairly quickly, or if, as with a vinegar, it should be stored on a shelf for flavor development. Simply follow the directions of the particular recipe you are executing and you should not have a problem.

Finally, many of these recipes may seem familiar to you even if you've never made them before. The art of cooking has been practiced for as long as humankind has inhabited this planet; there isn't much that hasn't already been tried by someone at some time in some place. These recipes find their roots in the basic procedures that cooks have used for years. Such procedures infuse a timelessness into recipes; only the ingredients change, as tastes and trends evolve into new cuisines. Feel free to play along—as you discover produce and spices you think could make an interesting condiment, substitute them for comparable ingredients within these pages. Cook with your mind as well as your palate, and, above all, enjoy yourself.

When I have my house I will suit myself
And have what I'll call my "condiment shelf"
Filled with all manner of herbs and spice,
Curry and chutney for meats and rice,
Pots and bottles of extracts rare—
Onions and garlic will both be there—
And soyo and saffron and savory-goo
And stuff that I'll buy from an old Hindu.
Ginger and syrup in quaint stone jars,
Almonds and figs in tinseled bars,
Astrakhan caviar, highly prized,
And citron and orange peel crystallized,
Anchovy paste and poha jam,
Basil and chili and marjoram,
Pickles and cheeses from every land,
And flavors that come from Samarkand;
And hung with a string from a handy hook
Will be a dog-eared, well thumbed book
That is pasted full of recipes
From France and Spain and the Caribees—
Roots and leaves and herbs to use
For curious soups and old ragouts.

Don Blanding
"Vagabond House"

The Art of Accompaniment

Chapter One

DRESSING UP: VINEGARS, OILS, DRESSINGS, AND MUSTARDS

"A loaf of bread" the Walrus said,
"Is what we chiefly need:
  Pepper and vinegar besides
  Are very good indeed—
  Now, if you're ready, Oysters dear,
  We can begin to feed."
        Lewis Carroll
        "The Walrus and the Carpenter"

Dressing up—isn't that what we do to food—dress it up to enhance the natural flavors? Millions of people dress up piping-hot sausages with spicy mustards and an endless variety of salads with oils, vinegars, and dressings. Hardly a home in the Western world doesn't contain a bottle or two of each. Undoubtedly, such dressings are a vital aspect of North American and European cuisine, and for good reason.

Historians tell us mustard has been around at least since Roman times, when mustard seeds were added to highly spiced sauces. In medieval Europe, cooks ground the seeds into a paste, variations of which have become in the twentieth century a multimillion-dollar industry for dozens of companies worldwide. Diners in Elizabethan England were traditionally served mustard alongside slabs of roasted porpoise.

Smooth and creamy Dijon, searing Chinese, crunchy German, and varietal wine and herb mustards are only a few of the many kinds available from today's grocer. The commercial variety is quite different from the product made at home. For high quality, commercial makers mix the ground mustard seed powder with liquid to mellow the seed's natural bitterness, then cook it at length to decrease the pungency; finally, extensive controlled aging develops the flavors. Some commercial makers don't cook their mustards at all; rather, a sophisticated milling process separates the hull from the interior and creates a mild powder. Neither of these methods can be duplicated precisely at home. Nevertheless, you can make a mouthwatering alternative, one that will keep your refrigerator, family, and friends well stocked with mustards for months, if not years.

About the same time the Romans experimented with mustard seed, they were also exploring the pleasures of flavored oils and vinegars, culinary secrets learned from the Greeks. Besides adding oil and vinegar to just about every dish served at their lusty banquets,

Roman cooks also used a layer of olive oil to preserve wine, and vinegar to pickle fruits and vegetables, much as we do today. Probably the most versatile of condiments, oil and vinegar go beyond the kitchen for many other household duties, such as disinfecting and polishing. But it is within the culinary domain that these time-honored condiments show their greatest talents. Just by being spiced, mixed with each other, or added to a wide variety of ingredients, they become entirely new products. Ever changing yet ever constant, oil and vinegar now enhance cuisines on nearly every continent around the globe.

Wine Vinegar

With patience and a little shelf space you can easily make your own wine vinegars. Depending on the grape variety of the wine used, homemade wine vinegars often have flavors unavailable in commercial products. This recipe can be doubled or tripled to use up leftover party wine.

Once you complete your first batch of wine vinegar, use it as a starter for future bottles. Use wine vinegar for any recipe (except canning recipes) calling for vinegar or lemon juice.

>*4 cups red or white wine*
>*1 1/3 to 2 cups red wine vinegar or white wine vinegar*

Use red wine with red wine vinegar and white with white. First check the acidity level on the wine vinegar label. If it is low—less than 5 percent acidity—use the greater quantity of vinegar in the recipe. If the acidity level is high—6 percent or higher—use the smaller amount.

Put the wine and vinegar in clean bottles, cap them, and store bottles on a cool, dark, dry shelf for at least four months. Check the vinegar each month thereafter (take a whiff). When the aroma becomes tart and pungent, yet still fruity, it is ready to use. This process can take as long as six months.

Makes 1 1/2 quarts, or less if a smaller amount of vinegar is used.

Cranberry Vinegar

The cranberry flavor is subtle, so combine this vinegar with plain vegetable oils as opposed to stronger olive and nut oils. Use it in marinades for poultry and game, or to dress a salad of fresh spinach leaves and watercress sprigs.

3½ cups red wine vinegar
1 teaspoon sugar
½ cup fresh cranberries

Combine the vinegar and sugar over high heat in a large saucepan. Pack the berries in a tall, clean quart bottle (or divide them among smaller bottles proportionally). When the vinegar mixture boils, pour it over the berries.

Cap the bottle and let the vinegar stand in a cool, dark spot at least one month before using. It gets significantly better with age. After several months, cranberry vinegar takes on a wonderful taste not comparable to other vinegars.

VARIATIONS

You may, if you wish, also make this vinegar with strawberries, cherries, raspberries, fresh currants, or any other dark and flavorful fruit. With these sweeter and less bitter fruits, adding sugar is not necessary.

Makes about 1 quart.

Garlic Vinegar

This vinegar mixed with some onion-scented oil makes an intriguing vinaigrette.

1 head of garlic, cloves separated, peeled, and halved
1 quart white or red wine vinegar

You may use either of two methods:

For the first method, add the garlic clove halves to the vinegar in its bottle, recap it, and let it sit on a shelf for two to three months. Check it every couple of weeks; when it reaches the intensity of flavor you wish, remove the cloves and begin to use.

The second method is considerably faster, but the result is a little less pungent. Bring the vinegar and garlic clove halves to a boil in a saucepan. Turn off heat. When the vinegar is cool, transfer it with the garlic to a tall, clean quart bottle (or into smaller bottles proportionally). Cap it and leave it on a shelf for at least a day. Check it every day until it reaches the intensity of flavor you wish. Remove the cloves and begin to use.

Makes 1 quart.

Ginger Rosemary Vinegar

I particularly like to use this vinegar to marinate meats, such as flank steak, for grilling. Combine equal parts of the vinegar and an oil, pour it over the meat, and marinate for at least two hours in the refrigerator.

> *1 quart white wine vinegar*
> *3 tablespoons peeled, chopped fresh gingerroot*
> *10 long, fresh rosemary sprigs*

In a large saucepan, heat the vinegar to a boil. Add the ginger and five rosemary sprigs. Turn off heat; let the mixture cool.

When the vinegar has reached room temperature, remove the ginger and rosemary. Pour the vinegar into a tall, clean quart bottle or several smaller bottles. Add the remaining rosemary sprigs proportionally; with the end of a long wooden spoon, completely submerge them. Cap and store on a cool, dark shelf for at least one week before using.

Makes 1 quart.

Lemon Vinegar

An unusual vinegar, with a tangy, citrus taste. Try substituting it whenever vinegar or lemon juice is called for in a recipe. Because it is strong, use less than you would of regular vinegar.

2 lemons, washed and sliced
2 cups white wine vinegar

Place the lemon slices in a quart jar (or, if you use smaller jars, divide them proportionally). Set this aside.

Bring the vinegar to a boil in a medium-sized saucepan. Pour the hot vinegar over the sliced lemons. Tightly cap jar.

Store the jar in a cool, dark place for two days. Discard lemons. Strain the vinegar through a cheesecloth-lined sieve. Return the vinegar to the jar or to a tall, clean bottle or several smaller bottles; cap and store on a cool, dark shelf. The vinegar is now ready to use.

Makes 2 cups.

Mint Vinegar

The perfect recipe for using all that wild mint overtaking the garden. Whisk with oil to make a vinaigrette for carrots that have been slightly poached and cooled, sliced tomatoes, or wild greens.

1 quart white wine vinegar
8 long, full sprigs of fresh peppermint, spearmint, or pineapple mint

Set the vinegar over high heat in a large saucepan. Meanwhile, wash and dry the mint.

When the vinegar boils, add four mint sprigs. Turn off heat. Let cool, uncovered, for half an hour, or until the vinegar reaches room temperature.

Remove the mint. Pour the vinegar into a tall, clean bottle or several smaller ones. Add the remaining mint sprigs proportionally; using the end of a long wooden spoon, completely submerge them. Cap bottles tightly.

Leave the vinegar in a cool, dark place for at least a week before using.

VARIATIONS

You may also use other herbs, such as oregano, basil, chervil, thyme, tarragon, or marjoram. A combination of herb sprigs makes a marvelous potpourri vinegar.

Makes 1 quart.

Pear Vinegar

Pear vinegar works best in recipes where its delicate flavor is not overwhelmed, such as for dressings and light sauces. It works splendidly in salads studded with slices of fresh pear or apple.

> *1 large firm pear, preferably Bosc or Anjou, peeled, quartered, and stemmed*
> *1 quart champagne or other white wine vinegar*

Place the pear in the bottom of a jar or bottle that holds at least 1½ quarts of liquid. Pour the vinegar over the pear. Cap the jar tightly.

Leave the jar in a cool, dark spot for two months. If you just can't wait, filter and transfer the vinegar to tall, clean bottles and begin to use after one month, but not before—the pear flavor needs time to develop.

Makes 1 quart.

Oil Piquante

Try substituting Oil *Piquante* whenever a recipe calls for vegetable oil. It adds a subtle bite to both sautéed and fried foods. For chile lovers, it makes the ultimate vinaigrette.

¼ cup sesame oil
1¾ cups vegetable oil
4 garlic cloves, halved and mashed with the side of a knife
1 tablespoon black peppercorns
1 cup dried chile pods

Combine the oils with the remaining ingredients in a 1-quart saucepan over medium heat. Partially cover. Heat until garlic turns a light golden color—about 10 minutes. Remove from heat, cover completely, and let cool.

Pick out the garlic; discard it. Pour the oil, peppercorns, and chile pods into a sterilized glass jar and cap it.

Store on a dark, cool shelf for two weeks before using. The longer it sits, the hotter it gets. For best results, let it sit at least one month.

Makes about 2½ cups.

Onion-Scented Oil

Ever so reminiscent of fragrant onions, this oil serves particularly well as a salad dressing base and for marinating meats.

2 cups virgin olive oil
3 cups sliced red onions or shallots

Combine the oil and onions or shallots in a large bowl. Cover with plastic wrap and leave in a cool place for 6 hours.

Remove the onions or shallots with a slotted spoon. (Serve them over grilled steaks or chicken.) Pour the oil into a jar; cap.

Makes 2 cups.

Oil Patricia

When I think of vanilla, I envision my friend Patricia Rain, author of *The Vanilla Cookbook*. One day, after we talked during an entire lunch about the hundreds of things a person can do with vanilla, I came up with this oil, my own best effort; the inspiration lies with Patricia. Use this whenever a recipe calls for oil, to add a subtle rich flavor.

1 cup vegetable oil (such as safflower, peanut, or corn)
1 cinnamon stick, broken into 3 pieces
1 whole nutmeg, broken in half (tap lightly with a hammer)
1 teaspoon whole cloves
1 vanilla bean

Combine the oil with the spices and vanilla bean in a saucepan. Over medium-high heat, cook the oil until the spices begin to crackle; continue cooking for 2 minutes. Turn off the heat, and let the oil cool to room temperature.

Pour the oil into a tall bottle. Add the spices and vanilla bean. Cap the bottle, and let the oil sit on a shelf for at least a week before using.

Makes 1 cup.

Aioli

For a luscious appetizer, set out a bowlful of *aioli* for dipping freshly cut-up vegetables or grilled prawns. You will be enjoying a time-honored condiment.

When the Duc de Richelieu was on the Spanish island of Minorca during the French-Spanish War of 1628, he copied this local sauce, and later he presented his own version, without the garlic, in Versailles. To honor Minorca's major city, Mahón, he called it mayonnaise.

1 thick slice French bread, crust removed	*2 egg yolks*
	¼ teaspoon salt
3 tablespoons milk	*1 cup virgin olive oil*
4 garlic cloves, pushed through a press	*1 tablespoon fresh lemon juice*
	2 tablespoons drained capers

Soak the bread in the milk in a small bowl for 5 minutes. Meanwhile, mash the garlic with a pestle in a medium-sized bowl. Squeeze all the milk out of the bread. Add the bread to the garlic, continuing to mash until smooth. Add the egg yolks one at a time, then the salt.

With a blender, food processor, or hand-held electric mixer, blend the mixture and slowly add the oil, *one drop at a time*. Stir down the mixture frequently to prevent oil buildup on the sides of the bowl. When all the oil has been incorporated, add the lemon juice and blend until thoroughly combined. Spoon the *aioli* into a bowl, and stir in the capers.

If not serving immediately, cover and refrigerate.

Makes 1⅓ cups.

Truffled Mayonnaise

If truffles in mayonnaise sounds decadent, you're right, it is. And such decadence . . .

3 dried truffles
2 egg yolks
¼ teaspoon salt
¾ teaspoon Dijon mustard

1 teaspoon truffle liquid (see below)
Dash white pepper
1 cup peanut oil
1 teaspoon white wine vinegar

Soak the dried truffles in boiling water to cover until they have plumped—about 3 hours. Drain the truffles and reserve one teaspoon of the truffle liquid. Mince the truffles, drain them again (press out water), and measure 3 tablespoons. Set this aside. Refrigerate leftover truffles for another use, such as stirring into a cream sauce, filling an omelette, or combining with wild rice.

Combine thoroughly the egg yolks, salt, mustard, truffle liquid, and white pepper; using a blender, food processor, or hand-held electric mixer, slowly add ¼ cup of the oil, *one drop at a time*. Keep the machine running and incorporate each drop before adding the next. Stir in ½ teaspoon vinegar. Add another ¼ cup of oil in the same manner as before, one drop at a time. Stir down mixture frequently.

Stir in the remaining vinegar, followed by the last ½ cup of oil; the last ½ cup can be added at a slightly faster rate, in a trickle. Be sure not to add too much at a time, or the mayonnaise will fall apart. After all the oil has been added, stir in the minced truffles.

If not serving immediately, cover and refrigerate.

Makes 1¼ cups.

Dill Mayonnaise

Homemade mayonnaise may be time consuming, but it is well worth the effort. You might try substituting for dill such other herbs as basil, tarragon, or thyme.

1 egg
2 egg yolks
¼ teaspoon dry mustard powder
½ teaspoon salt

2 teaspoons fresh lemon juice
1 cup safflower or sunflower oil
1 tablespoon minced fresh dill

In a blender, a food processor, or a medium-sized bowl with a hand-held mixer, blend the egg, egg yolks, mustard powder, and salt. When smooth, add the lemon juice.

With the machine running again, add the oil, *one drop at a time.* If you add too much at a time, the mayonnaise will fall apart; so take your time, blending each drop thoroughly before adding the next. Stop occasionally and stir down the sides, to prevent oil buildup. After all the oil has been incorporated, stir in the fresh dill.

If not serving immediately, cover and refrigerate.

Makes 1 cup.

N'Orleans Mayonnaise

The perfect accompaniment to cold meats, sandwiches, and artichokes—Creole spices give it a discernible Southern taste.

1 egg yolk
1 tablespoon cider vinegar
½ teaspoon Dijon mustard
¼ teaspoon salt
¼ teaspoon filé powder
¼ teaspoon dried thyme
¼ teaspoon dried basil

¼ teaspoon dried oregano
⅛ teaspoon garlic powder
⅛ teaspoon paprika
⅛ teaspoon white pepper
⅛ teaspoon Tabasco sauce
Dash cayenne pepper
⅔ cup safflower oil

With a blender, food processor, or an electric hand-held mixer, combine the egg yolk with the vinegar, mustard, and seasonings. With the machine running, add the oil, *one drop at a time*, until only ¼ cup of oil remains. Stop the machine and stir down the sides.

Turn on the machine again and add the last ¼ cup of oil, a half-teaspoonful at a time. If as you add the oil by the half-teaspoonful, the mayonnaise begins to look stringy, it is on the verge of separating. Return to one-drop-at-a-time additions.

If not serving immediately, cover and refrigerate.

Makes ¾ cup.

Berry Dressing

The perfect match for a watercress and feta salad. (If you use *Cranberry Vinegar*, be sure to substitute lighter vegetable oil for the virgin olive oil.)

¼ cup berry vinegar (see page 6)
½ cup virgin olive oil
1 egg yolk
½ teaspoon salt
¼ teaspoon dry mustard powder
¼ teaspoon ground ginger
Salt

Combine the ingredients in a 12-ounce jar with a tight-fitting lid. Shake vigorously until well blended. Taste and, if desired, adjust the salt.

Use immediately or refrigerate until ready to use.

Makes about ¾ cup.

Emerald Mint Vinaigrette

Best over a salad of fresh garden greens, preferably ones that do not compete with the dressing.

½ cup corn oil
2 tablespoons Mint Vinegar
    (see page 10)
2 tablespoons chopped fresh
    mint
1 garlic clove

⅛ teaspoon freshly ground
    pepper
1 pinch salt
1 pinch ground cumin
1 pinch dry mustard powder

Combine the ingredients in a small blender. Blend until the garlic completely disappears and the mixture is creamy and frothy.

Serve immediately or refrigerate until ready to use.

Makes a little more than ½ cup.

Cilantro Lime Dressing

Pour over a salad of mixed greens, avocado, jicama, and oranges.

¼ cup virgin olive oil
2 tablespoons peanut oil
½ cup fresh lime juice
1 tablespoon minced fresh
   cilantro

¼ teaspoon dried oregano
Dash cayenne pepper
Freshly ground pepper
Salt

Combine all ingredients in a 12-ounce jar with a tight-fitting lid. Shake vigorously until well blended. Serve immediately or refrigerate until ready to use.

Makes about ¾ cup.

Balsamic Vanilla Dressing

Vanilla in a salad dressing? Mismatched as it may seem, vanilla adds a smooth, balanced character to even the simplest set of ingredients. Serve over sliced, ripe tomatoes.

¾ cup safflower oil
¼ cup balsamic vinegar
1 tablespoon white wine vinegar
¼ teaspoon vanilla extract
⅛ teaspoon ground nutmeg

Combine the ingredients in a 2-cup container with a tight-fitting lid. Shake vigorously, blending well. Serve immediately or refrigerate until ready to use.

Makes about 1 cup.

Chinese Sesame Dressing

I like to serve this dressing with a salad of cold, sliced duck, green onions, water chestnuts, lettuce, and a fresh tropical fruit, such as papaya.

¼ cup plus 1 tablespoon peanut oil
¼ cup rice vinegar
1 tablespoon fresh lime juice
1 teaspoon sesame seeds

½ teaspoon light soy sauce
¼ teaspoon sesame oil
¼ teaspoon sugar
⅛ teaspoon freshly ground black pepper

Whisk the ingredients together until well blended. Toss immediately with salad.

Makes about ⅔ cup.

Madeleine Kamman's Mango and Rum Dressing

In her book *In Madeleine's Kitchen*, Madeleine Kamman describes serving this rich and thick dressing over a salad of lobster, shrimp, butter lettuce, papaya, and kiwi fruit. Mrs. Kamman recommends lightly brushing only the fruit in the salad with dressing. I like it on the seafood as well.

1 very ripe mango, peeled and pitted
2 tablespoons rum
2 tablespoons fresh lime juice
2 tablespoons fresh lemon juice
1½ teaspoons dried mint, powdered
1 teaspoon lime zest
½ teaspoon vanilla extract
1 small garlic clove, mashed with the side of a knife
⅛ teaspoon cayenne pepper
½ cup virgin olive oil
Salt

Place the mango pulp in a blender or food processor with all ingredients but the olive oil and salt. Blend until smooth. With the machine running, slowly pour in the oil. Add salt to taste.

Refrigerate dressing for 1 hour before serving. Because mango can ferment with the slightest heat, keep refrigerated until ready to use.

Makes about 1½ cups.

Papaya Seed Dressing

What in the world should you do with Papaya Seed Dressing? Try topping slices of ripe avocados and beefsteak tomatoes.

½ cup peanut oil
¼ cup white wine vinegar
¼ cup fresh papaya
2 tablespoons papaya seeds
(scooped from fresh
papaya)

1 teaspoon sugar
¼ teaspoon ground ginger
¼ teaspoon whole green
peppercorns
⅛ teaspoon salt
⅛ teaspoon curry powder

In a blender or food processor, blend the oil and vinegar. With the machine running, drop in the papaya. When pureed, add papaya seeds. Continue processing until the seeds appear mainly as flecks. Add the remaining ingredients. Blend just until thick and creamy.

Serve immediately or refrigerate a few hours until ready to use.

Makes 1¼ cups.

Shallot Vinaigrette Parmesan

Toss with a fresh vegetable salad of sliced red, green, and yellow bell peppers, a stalk of thinly sliced celery, and a thinly sliced carrot.

⅔ cup virgin olive oil
¼ cup peanut oil
¼ cup herb vinegar (see page 10)
1 egg yolk
¼ cup minced shallots
2 tablespoons grated Parmesan cheese

1 garlic clove, minced
1 teaspoon fresh lemon juice
½ teaspoon dry mustard powder
⅛ teaspoon freshly ground black pepper
Salt

Combine all ingredients in a 12-ounce jar with a tight-fitting lid. Shake vigorously until well blended.

Serve immediately or refrigerate until ready to use.

Makes about 1¼ cups.

Banana and Guava Dressing for Fruit

Getting tired of plain fruit salad? Try dressing up slices of peaches, nectarines, apricots, and halved strawberries with this dressing for a tropical extravaganza.

1 cup sliced bananas
½ cup guava nectar
¼ cup plain yogurt
1 teaspoon honey

Mix the ingredients in a blender or food processor until a smooth puree. Serve immediately over fresh fruit.

Makes 1¼ cups.

Hazelnut Sherry Vinaigrette
with Gorgonzola

The perfect complement to mixed greens or sliced tomatoes.

*⅓ cup plus 2 tablespoons
   safflower oil
3 tablespoons sherry vinegar
   (less, if particularly
   strong)
1 teaspoon hazelnut oil*

*¼ cup crumbled Gorgonzola,
   Roquefort, or other blue
   cheese
1 egg yolk
Salt and freshly ground pepper*

Combine all ingredients in a 12-ounce jar with a tight-fitting lid.
Shake vigorously until well blended. Serve immediately.

Makes ¾ cup.

Creamy Adriatic Feta Dressing

Try this over a salad of diced cucumbers, tomatoes, green olives, bell pepper, and sliced scallions. If possible, use Bulgarian feta—it's milder and smoother and feels buttery on the tongue. Additional salt is not necessary—whether you use Bulgarian or Greek feta, the cheese contains enough to flavor the dressing.

⅓ cup crumbled feta cheese
¼ cup sour cream
¼ cup unflavored yogurt

1 tablespoon chopped fresh dill
1 tablespoon whole milk
Freshly ground black pepper to taste

Combine all ingredients in a blender or food processor. Pulse a couple of times, barely mixing ingredients; dressing should be a little chunky. (If you prefer a smooth puree, however, by all means pulse away.)

Serve immediately.

Makes ¾ cup.

Moroccan Orange Flower Dressing

Spoon over a platter of sliced ripe avocados and crisp radishes. Top with chopped parsley.

3 tablespoons safflower oil
3 tablespoons fresh orange juice
2 tablespoons fresh lemon juice
½ teaspoon sugar

1 tablespoon orange flower water (available in Middle Eastern markets and international grocery stores)

Combine all ingredients in a 12-ounce jar with a tight-fitting lid. Shake vigorously to blend well.

Refrigerate 1 hour to combine flavors.

Makes about ½ cup.

Chutney Cream for Chicken Salad

The next time you have leftover roast chicken, duck, or turkey, chop it and some celery and apples, and toss with Chutney Cream. You will never use mayonnaise again—even homemade—on such a salad.

> ¼ cup heavy cream
> 1 tablespoon Golden Pear Chutney (see page 81)
> 1 tablespoon whole milk
> 2 teaspoons Dijon mustard
> 1 teaspoon dry sherry

In a blender or food processor, blend the ingredients until smooth. Serve immediately or refrigerate until ready to use.

Makes about ½ cup.

Asian Ginger Dressing for Seafood

In the middle of summer, when the heat refuses to subside even late at night and the cool breezes selfishly hide off the shorelines, a seafood salad can refresh the spirit as well as the palate. Poach your favorite fish or shellfish; chill it 2 to 3 hours in the refrigerator. Break it apart and mix it with chopped fresh vegetables. Toss with dressing and a few sesame seeds. Serve with a spicy wine, such as Gewürztraminer, and a hunk of chewy French bread.

3 tablespoons mayonnaise
2 tablespoons sunflower oil
2 teaspoons rice vinegar
    (available in Asian
    markets)
1 teaspoon fresh lemon juice
1 teaspoon minced fresh
    ginger
½ teaspoon soy sauce
½ teaspoon sesame oil

Mix the ingredients together in a small blender or food processor until smooth and creamy. Transfer the dressing to a jar; cover and refrigerate 1 hour before tossing with salad.

This makes a fairly thick dressing. If a thinner consistency is desired, blend in 1 or 2 more tablespoons of sunflower oil.

Makes about ⅓ cup.

Tarragon Buttermilk Dressing

In summer, use fresh tarragon instead of dried; the flavor is much better. Serve as a dipping sauce for crudités or with a salad of fresh spinach and watercress.

⅓ cup buttermilk
⅓ cup sour cream
¼ cup minced fresh parsley
1 tablespoon mayonnaise
4 teaspoons fresh or 2 teaspoons dried tarragon

1 teaspoon drained capers
¼ teaspoon minced rosemary
⅛ teaspoon ground green peppercorns
Dash white pepper

Whisk all ingredients together in a small bowl. Cover and refrigerate for 1 hour to allow flavors to blend.

Makes about 1 cup.

Avocado Basil Cream with Capers

Serve alongside a platter of cold, sliced summer squashes and cauliflower and broccoli flowerets.

¼ cup cubed ripe avocado
¼ cup virgin olive oil
2 tablespoons chopped fresh basil
1 tablespoon fresh lemon juice

1 tablespoon whole milk
1 tablespoon heavy cream
½ teaspoon caper liquid (from jar of capers)
1 teaspoon drained capers

In a small blender or food processor, combine the avocado, oil, basil, and lemon juice. Blend until smooth. Add the milk, cream, and caper liquid, and blend just until mixed. Transfer the dressing to a bowl. Stir in the capers.

Use immediately or refrigerate until ready to use.

Makes ½ cup.

Walnut Cassis Dressing for Asparagus

No vegetable marks the onset of spring as do delicate, green stalks of asparagus, crisp and fragrant with the scent of rich soil and warm afternoons. To best appreciate the season's first bounty, poach and chill as much as desired and dress with the blend below.

⅓ cup peanut oil
1 tablespoon walnut oil
2 teaspoons white wine
*   vinegar*
2 teaspoons fresh lemon juice
¾ teaspoon crème de cassis
*   liqueur*

Pinch ground cinnamon
Salt
Freshly ground green
*   peppercorns*
1 tablespoon minced walnuts

Combine all ingredients in a 12-ounce jar with a tight-fitting lid. Shake vigorously until well blended.

Makes ½ cup.

Sweet 'n' Spiced Mustard

This sweet, pungent mustard goes particularly well with grilled sausages and cold, sliced meats.

2 cups dry mustard powder	½ cup "runny" honey
1¼ cups white wine vinegar	¼ teaspoon ground cinnamon
3 eggs, beaten	¼ teaspoon ground cloves
1¼ cups brown sugar, packed	¼ teaspoon ground nutmeg

Whisk the dry mustard and vinegar together until smooth and creamy. Set the mixture aside for 1 hour.

Transfer the mustard and vinegar to the top of a double boiler. Whisk in the remaining ingredients, beating until no lumps remain. Over simmering water, cook, stirring frequently, until thickened—20 to 25 minutes. Be sure to stir down the sides during cooking.

Pour the mustard into clean jars. Cap and refrigerate. Keeps several months in refrigerator.

Makes about 3⅓ cups.

Beer Mustard

Smooth and chunky in texture; orange-brown in color. Hot and sweet! Use this mustard sparingly with sandwiches, grilled sausages, or cold, sliced meats, or spread over steaks before broiling.

1 cup dry mustard powder
⅔ cup strong-flavored beer or ale
¼ cup molasses
¼ teaspoon salt

⅛ teaspoon ground turmeric
½ cup minced dried peaches or apricots
1 tablespoon minced candied ginger

Mix together the mustard powder and beer. Set this aside for a half-hour.

Stir in the remaining ingredients. To preserve the mustard by refrigerating, simply spoon it into clean jars and cap them before refrigerating. Keeps several months in the refrigerator. If you wish to store the mustard on the shelf, spoon it into 2 sterilized, still-hot, ¾-pint jars. Process it in a boiling water bath for 10 minutes. Wipe the rim, and cap immediately with a still-hot lid, plus ring.

Makes 3 cups.

Chapter Two

RELISHING THE PICKLE

On a hot day in Virginia, I know of nothing more
comforting than a fine spiced pickle, brought up
troutlike from the sparkling depths of the aromatic
jar below the stairs in Aunt Sally's cellar.

Thomas Jefferson

Pickle expert Leonard Louis Levinson (*The Complete Book of Pickles and Relishes*) offers a wealth of pickle trivia. Were you aware Cleopatra ate pickles because she believed they would enhance her looks and preserve her health? Emperor Tiberius was another pickle aficionado, as were Washington, Adams, and Jefferson. But these last are no surprise. In the harsh winters of the American colonies, fresh vegetables were scarce. Pickles often afforded the only opportunity to eat produce at all, which also is why troops of every army since Roman times have consumed extraordinary quantities of them. During World War II, for example, 40 percent of the U.S. pickle production went to the men in uniform.

No doubt about it—pickles have been and will continue to be one of the world's favorite foods. Hardly a country lacks a preferred version, as the selection in this chapter illustrates.

Pickling itself is a craft in method (see the appendix, A Word About Canning, before canning pickles for shelf storage) and, in the ingredients you combine, an art. You can pickle almost anything, with any number of methods, using an endless variety of brines, vinegars, spices, and herbs—as long as you follow these basic guidelines:

- Use only freshly picked vegetables and fruits, free of bruising. Purchase or pick them ripe and firm, not mushy.
- Vinegars should contain 4 to 6 percent acetic acid. This is the equivalent of 40 to 60 grain, as specified on commercial labels. A vinegar of less than 4 percent acetic acid will not properly pickle; spoilage may occur. Do not use the homemade wine vinegar from chapter 1 for pickling, because you cannot positively ascertain its acetic acid content.
- White distilled, white wine, and champagne vinegars retain the natural colors of foods you pickle. Cider, malt, sherry, and red

wine vinegars darken foods, as well as adding distinctive flavors.

· When preparing a hot vinegar brine, do not boil the solution for more than 1 minute unless the recipe says to; boiling decreases the vinegar's acetic acid level.

· Any table salt will work, though I prefer natural sea salt.

· Do not use salt or sugar substitutes.

· Use utensils made only of glass, aluminum, stainless steel, clay, enamel, or plastic. Avoid using copper, iron, brass, or galvanized utensils—they can discolor foods and in some cases cause toxic poisoning.

· Any of the pickles processed in a hot boiling water bath may be refrigerated instead. This alternate method produces a much crisper pickle, but takes up precious refrigerator space.

· Store all pickles canned for shelf storage in a cool, dark, dry spot.

· Last, but of great importance: do not change the salt, sugar, or vinegar amounts unless you are doubling a recipe. They are vital to proper preservation. If you are concerned about sugar or salt intake, you can make pickles simply by immersing cut-up vegetables and fruits in straight vinegar for 2 to 3 days and refrigerate. The effect is quite pungent, but it is salt and sugar free.

Peter Piper's Sweet Pickled Peppers

I like to keep a jar of these around for rainy days when I don't feel like doing much in the kitchen. They are great with ham sandwiches, smorgasbords, and pork chops.

5 large bell peppers, preferably different colors, seeded and quartered
Boiling water
2 cups sugar
2 cups white distilled vinegar
2 cups water
1 teaspoon salt
1 small yellow onion, peeled and sliced
4 garlic cloves

Pack the peppers into four sterilized, still-hot pint jars. Cover each jar's peppers with boiling water and let stand 5 minutes.

Combine the sugar, vinegar, water, and salt in a medium-sized saucepan. Heat these to boiling; simmer 5 minutes.

Drain the water from the peppers. Add the onion slices and garlic cloves to the jars; pack them tightly. Pour the boiling vinegar brine over the vegetables. Wipe rims and cap immediately with still-hot lids, plus rings. Process in a boiling water bath for 10 minutes.

Let the pickles sit on a cool, dark shelf for one week before using. Refrigerate after opening.

Makes 4 pints.

Tarragon Asparagus Pickles

These crunchy, tarragon-laced gems make a wonderful light appetizer prior to a cool summer meal. Try serving them with a dip of homemade mayonnaise, Dijon mustard, and a little *Harissa* sauce (p. 212).

2 ¼ cups white distilled vinegar
⅓ cup white wine vinegar
2 ¼ cups water
3 tablespoons salt
16 full sprigs fresh tarragon
2 pounds tender, young asparagus, preferably thin stalks

2 small shallots, each partially split in half
2 garlic cloves, each partially split in half
2 teaspoons juniper berries (or if unavailable, mustard seeds)

Combine the vinegars, water, and salt in a saucepan over high heat. While this is coming to a boil, put eight tarragon sprigs in the bottom of each of two sterilized, still-hot quart jars. Trim the asparagus of any white ends and pack them in the jars. Allow ½ inch headspace. Nestle one shallot and one garlic clove in each jar. Put 1 teaspoon of juniper berries (or mustard seeds) in each jar, as well.

Pour boiling vinegar brine into the jars, and cap them tightly. Let the jars cool; when they are room temperature, store them in the refrigerator. Chill for one week before opening.

You can also use sterilized jars and lids, process the quarts in a boiling water bath for 20 minutes, and store them on a cool, dark shelf. The asparagus will be less crunchy.

Makes 2 quarts.

Sassy Texas Okra

There's only one way to eat these fiery little pickles—straight. I love to snack on them with icy-cold ale.

2 pounds fresh okra
2⅔ cups cider vinegar
1⅓ cups water
1½ tablespoons salt
4 garlic cloves, slightly crushed
  with the side of a knife

4 dried chile pods
4 small bay leaves
2 tablespoons Pickling Spices
  (p. 216)

Trim ¹⁄₁₆ inch from the stem end of each okra. Set okra aside.

Combine vinegar, water, and salt in a saucepan over high heat. While this is coming to a boil, put one garlic clove, one chile pod, one bay leaf, and ½ tablespoon of pickling spices in the bottom of each of four sterilized, still-hot pint jars. Tightly pack in one layer of okra, wide end down. Add a second layer, pointed end down. Push down hard to pack okra together tightly; this is important, so that okra won't float to the tops of the jars after processing.

Pour boiling vinegar brine into the filled jars. Wipe rims and cap immediately with still-hot lids, plus rings. Process 10 minutes in a boiling water bath.

Store on a cool shelf for at least one month before opening.

Makes 4 pints.

Refrigerator Green Bean Dills

Every summer my stepdaughters, Jana and Julie, pester me to make these pickles. The two of them can finish off a jar in less than 20 minutes.

1¼ cups white distilled vinegar
¼ cup white wine vinegar
1½ cups water
2 tablespoons salt
1 pound tender, young green beans, trimmed

5 garlic cloves
1 teaspoon mustard seed
1 teaspoon dried chile flakes
5 sprigs fresh dill weed

Combine the vinegars, water, and salt in a saucepan over high heat. While the brine is coming to a boil, pack a sterilized, still-hot quart jar with beans, garlic, mustard seed, chile flakes, and dill weed. Cover with the hot vinegar brine. Cap immediately.

Cool the jar to room temperature, and transfer it to the refrigerator. Keep chilled at least two weeks before serving. Best when pickled for one month.

Makes 1 quart.

Pickled Green Beans and Carrots

Try serving these as an appetizer before a garlic-laden dinner party. Balance the plate with less pungent items, such as olives, miniature pickled corn on the cob, and sticks of jicama.

6 cups water
3 cups cider vinegar
3 tablespoons salt
6 sprigs fresh dill weed
6 fresh jalapeño chile peppers,
    tops trimmed, split in half
6 garlic cloves, halved

1½ pounds green beans,
    trimmed
¾ pound carrots, trimmed,
    peeled, halved lengthwise
    and quartered
    horizontally
3 teaspoons mustard seed
3 teaspoons dill seed

Combine water, vinegar, and salt in a 3-quart pot over high heat. While this is coming to a boil, lay three sterilized still-hot quart jars on their sides and pack each in the following order: one dill weed sprig, two chile halves, two garlic halves, one-third of the beans, one-third of the carrots, two chile halves, two garlic halves, one dill weed sprig, 1 teaspoon mustard seed, and 1 teaspoon dill seed. Cover the packed contents of upright jars with boiling vinegar brine, leaving ½ inch headspace. Wipe rims and cap immediately with still-hot lids, plus rings.

Process 20 minutes in a boiling water bath. Do not open for one month.

Makes 3 quarts.

Alta Vista Marinated Carrots

On a recent visit to Southern California, I went with friends to the Alta Vista, a homey little restaurant in San Diego's Old Town where tourists remain scarce and locals relax with obscure Mexican beer and mariachi guitar music. I couldn't stop eating the appetizer of marinated carrots, a peppery pickle served in many Mexican restaurants. What I like most about owner Mary Sargent's recipe is the subtle spicing—her method allows the sweet taste of the carrots to burst through. Also, since they don't sear your taste buds, you can eat a lot of them.

2 pounds carrots, peeled and
    sliced on the diagonal ¼
    inch thick
1½ quarts warm water
Whole jalapeño peppers from 2
    (3.5-ounce) cans, with
    liquid

2 yellow onions, peeled and
    sliced
1 tablespoon dried oregano
6 whole garlic cloves
2 cups apple cider vinegar
¼ cup vegetable oil
2 bay leaves
1 tablespoon salt

Place the carrots in a 3- or 4-quart pot. Add the warm water, partially cover the pot, and bring it to a boil over high heat. Cook at a hard boil 5 minutes; remove from heat. Add the peppers and their liquid, sliced onions, oregano, garlic, vinegar, oil, bay leaves, and salt. Cover, and let cool for several hours.

Taste the carrots. If the flavor is hot enough for you, transfer just the carrots, onions, and garlic to two clean quart jars. If you prefer the pickles considerably spicier—trust me, they can get really hot—don't exclude the peppers from the jars. In this case, you will need an additional pint jar. Cover the contents with cooking liquid, and cap with clean lids.

Store the pickles in the refrigerator for three days before serving. They keep for a week or so after opening.

Makes about 9 cups.

Puckering Pearls

Serve with picnic fare—especially sausages and beer.

1 pound pearl onions
½ cup salt
3 cups cider vinegar
1 tablespoon brown sugar, packed
1 cinnamon stick
1 small nutmeg, cracked open (tap carefully with a hammer)

2 teaspoons whole cloves
1 tablespoon juniper berries
1 teaspoon green peppercorns
¼ teaspoon ground mace
2 sprigs fresh tarragon

The day before making the pickles, plunge the onions in a pot of boiling water for 1 minute; drain them in a colander. Use a knife to slip off the peels and cut off the onions' tops and bottoms.

Lay the prepared onions on a cookie sheet. Sprinkle them with salt and leave them overnight.

Combine the vinegar, sugar, and spices—all seasonings but the tarragon—in a medium-sized saucepan. Bring them to a boil. Cover, remove from heat, and let sit overnight.

The next morning, rinse and drain the onions. Bring the vinegar solution back to a boil. Put the tarragon sprigs in the bottom of two sterilized, still-hot pint jars. Pack in the onions, and cover them with the boiling vinegar solution. Wipe rims and cap immediately with still-hot lids, plus rings. Process for 10 minutes in a boiling water bath.

Store one month before using.

Makes 2 pints.

Kim Chee

[KOREAN VEGETABLE PICKLE]

Kim chee goes best with Asian dishes; however you serve it, present diners with only small amounts to start: it is particularly hot.

⅔ pound Chinese cabbage (also known as Napa cabbage)
½ pound daikon radish, peeled and sliced diagonally, ¼ inch thick
1 medium cucumber, peeled and sliced diagonally, ¼ inch thick
1 medium turnip, peeled and sliced diagonally, ¼ inch thick
½ cup salt
3 green onions, sliced
3 garlic cloves, pushed through a press
4 teaspoons peeled and minced fresh gingerroot
1 tablespoon dried chile flakes
2 teaspoons soy sauce
1 tablespoon salt
1 cup water

Layer whole cabbage leaves, sliced daikon, cucumber, and turnip in a large bowl. Between layers, liberally sprinkle ½ cup of salt. Cover the vegetables with water, and set a wide, heavy plate or lid on top to completely submerge them. Leave overnight or at least 12 hours.

Drain the vegetables in a colander. Using a very sharp knife, julienne each vegetable to a uniform size. Return them to the large bowl, and add green onions, pressed garlic, gingerroot, chile flakes, soy sauce, salt, and 1 cup water. Toss to combine.

Spoon the vegetables with liquid into a large crock or a couple of clean jars. Cover tightly or cap; refrigerate for three days before opening. Every day, turn jars upside down a couple of times to distribute spices, or stir vegetables in the crock.

Makes about 1½ quarts.

Tsukemono

Like *kim chee*, this is a condiment that goes best with Asian dishes. But it also goes quite well with sandwiches or simply served as a first course to dinner.

2½ pounds green cabbage or
    Chinese (Napa) cabbage,
    julienned
2 green onions, sliced
6 cups rice vinegar
2 tablespoons fresh lemon juice
½ cup sugar (increase if you
    like a sweeter pickle)
¼ teaspoon soy sauce
1 cup water
1 tablespoon salt

Place the julienned cabbage and onions in a large bowl or crock. Bring the remaining ingredients to a boil in a large pot. Pour the boiling vinegar brine over the vegetables, and set a wide, heavy plate or lid on top to completely submerge them. Cover the bowl with a tea towel and store it in a cool spot for 24 to 36 hours.

In summer, the cabbage will pickle in about two days; in winter, pickling takes longer. Simply check the cabbage each day. When it reaches the degree of tartness you prefer, transfer it to large jars, cap, and keep refrigerated. Keeps for several weeks.

Makes a little more than 2 quarts.

Sour Tomatoes

The hallmark of a good Jewish deli has always been a crock of kosher-style pickles and sour green tomatoes on every table. These tart and beloved accoutrements are as much a part of Jewish cuisine as lox, bagels, and cream cheese.

5 full sprigs fresh dill weed
1 tablespoon dill seed
1 teaspoon black peppercorns
2 garlic cloves, halved
1 dried chile pod
1 bay leaf

2 ¼ pounds firm green tomatoes (preferably 1 ½ inch in diameter—larger ones can be halved)
6 cups water
3 ¾ cups white distilled vinegar
1 cup salt

Pack the dill weed, seasonings, and tomatoes in a large bowl or crock, in the order listed. Bring the water, vinegar, and salt to a boil, and pour the boiling vinegar brine over the tomatoes. Set a wide, heavy plate or pot on top to completely submerge them.

Cover the bowl or crock with a tea towel and store it in a cool spot for five to seven days. If froth appears on top, remove it with a shallow spoon. Check the tomatoes every day. When ready, liquid will begin to appear cloudy and tomatoes will taste sour. If they start to wrinkle, don't worry; they are okay to use—but don't leave them any longer.

Transfer the sour tomatoes to three sterilized pint jars. Cover the tomatoes with the liquid, cap them, and refrigerate them to stop the pickling process.

Keeps several weeks in the refrigerator.

Makes 3 pints.

Cornichons

These are the divine little pickles that *charcuteries*, French cafés, and bistros serve alongside pâté, sliced meats, and salads. Tiny cucumbers can be difficult to find. Your best bets are to grow a plant in the backyard or locate a farm where you can pick them yourself. Either way allows you the exact size you want and ensures their freshness—and allows you to make a lot of them, because of the low cost.

3 pounds tiny pickling cucumbers, 1 to 1½ inches in length

6 small sprigs fresh tarragon

6 small sprigs fresh marjoram or oregano

3 teaspoons juniper berries (or if unavailable, mustard seeds)

3 teaspoons whole green peppercorns

4½ cups red wine vinegar or champagne vinegar

1¾ cups water

1½ tablespoons salt

1½ tablespoons sugar

Using a stiff vegetable brush under running water, scrub off the tiny thorns on the cucumbers. Set aside cucumbers to drain.

Sterilize six pint jars. In the bottom of each, lay the following ingredients: 1 tarragon sprig, 1 marjoram or oregano sprig, ½ teaspoon juniper berries (or mustard seed), and ½ teaspoon green peppercorns. Now tightly pack in the tiny cucumbers, vertically. When you think you can't get in even one extra cucumber, keep pushing in more.

Over high heat, bring the vinegar, water, salt, and sugar to a boil. Pour the boiling vinegar brine into the packed jars. Wipe rims and cap immediately with still-hot lids, plus rings.

Process 5 minutes in a boiling water bath. Store jars on a cool, dark shelf for at least two weeks before opening. Alternatively, if you would like the pickles extra crisp, delete the water bath and refrigerate them instead.

Makes 6 pints.

Fourth-Generation Recipe for Dills

In the small Northern California town of Lodi, the Phillips family has worked a farm for four generations. Over the years, the operation has grown to include a winery, a small restaurant, and a produce stand with sixty-nine different kinds of fruits and vegetables. Customers from all over adore the pickles that Jeanne Phillips proudly notes her family has been making since the farm began.

*3 to 6 pounds freshly picked
   cucumbers
For each jar:
   2 garlic cloves
   1 sprig fresh dill weed,
      including head
   3 fresh grape leaves*

*1 fresh hot chile pepper
   (optional)
For brine:
   ½ gallon nonsoftened
      water
   ½ cup noniodized salt
   1¼ cups cider vinegar*

The number of pounds of cucumbers this recipe will pickle depends on the size of the cucumbers. Generally, allow 16 medium-sized cucumbers per quart jar. If you run short of vinegar brine, simply make more. If you have too much, use it to make other vegetable pickles or refrigerate it for later use.

Pack freshly picked cucumbers into still-hot, sterilized quart jars with the garlic cloves, fresh dill weed, and grape leaves distributed in the bottoms, middles, and tops of jars. Also add the hot chile pepper to each jar, if you wish.

Combine the nonsoftened water, noniodized salt, and cider vinegar over high heat. When this boils, pour it over the cucumbers in jars. Seal with hot, sterilized lids.

Turn the jars upside down for several hours, then keep them in a cool spot for a minimum of one week before eating. Sometimes they overflow as they ferment, but they usually reseal. If any jars don't reseal, use them in the first couple of months. Sealed jars will keep several months on a cool shelf.

Makes 1 or more quarts.

Marinated Artichokes

In California, marinating is only one of dozens of ways we prepare the popular artichoke. Eat these pickles fairly soon after making them. They will last a few days in the refrigerator, but they may get excessively strong and overwhelm the artichoke's distinctive flavor.

3 cups water
3 cups vinegar (white distilled, cider, or wine)
1½ pounds small artichokes or artichoke hearts
1 tablespoon salt

5 dried chile pods
3 large garlic cloves, halved
¼ cup fresh herbs, such as oregano and basil
¾ cup sherry or wine vinegar
1 cup virgin olive oil

Put the water and 3 cups of vinegar in a 3-quart pot near the sink.

Remove the tough outer leaves from the artichokes. Peel the bases down to the tender, light-green leaves. Slice off dark-colored tops and bottoms. Slice the artichokes in half lengthwise; remove the choke—any inner purple leaves or fuzz. Place each artichoke in the vinegar solution immediately after trimming (otherwise, artichokes will badly discolor).

Add the salt and chile pods to the pot, cover it, and set it over high heat. When it boils, reduce the heat to medium high and continue cooking the artichokes until tender—10 to 15 minutes. Drain, discard vinegar brine, and allow the artichokes to cool.

Put the garlic cloves and fresh herbs in a large bowl, plastic container, or jar. Add the cooled artichokes. Cover them with the sherry or wine vinegar and olive oil, and cap.

Refrigerate the artichokes at least 24 hours before using. Stir them or turn the jar upside down a couple of times a day to distribute flavors.

The olive oil may congeal in the refrigerator after a while. If this happens, take the jar out of the refrigerator and let it sit on a kitchen shelf for a couple of hours before serving.

Makes 1 ½ pounds.

Fig Pickles

[FROM LUCILLE MAYO SMALLEY
OF SANTA ROSA, CALIFORNIA]

I admit to having culinary prejudices, and one of them is against pickled fruits, despite my adoration of fruit chutneys. So when a friend, Charlotte Brown, insisted I try her aunt's fig pickles, I was a little less than enthusiastic. But I also don't like to hurt people's feelings; I accepted the jar and promised Charlotte I would try one. These pickles turned out to be the best figs I've ever eaten. I'm embarrassed to say I finished off the jar in less than a week.

4 quarts (½ peck) medium-sized fresh, firm, dark figs	3 cups white wine vinegar
2 quarts water	1 tablespoon whole cloves
5 cups packed brown sugar	1 tablespoon whole allspice
	3 sticks cinnamon

Place the figs in a large bowl. Bring 2 quarts of water to a boil and pour it over the figs. Leave them to cool.

When the figs are room temperature, transfer them with a slotted spoon to a second bowl. Pour the fig liquid into a large (at least 4-quart) pot. Add 3 cups of the brown sugar and the vinegar, and bring the vinegar solution to a boil. Continue boiling it until the sugar dissolves completely. Let the solution stand until cool.

Add the figs to the cooled solution, and bring it to a slow boil. Partially cover, and cook 30 minutes. Add the rest of the sugar and, tied in several layers of cheesecloth, the spices. Continue boiling slowly until figs appear almost translucent. Remove and discard spices. Turn off the heat and let figs stand 12 hours in a cool spot.

Reheat the figs and solution to a simmer. Pack the figs and solution into sterilized, still-hot quart jars. Wipe rims and cap immediately with still-hot lids, plus rings. Process for 35 minutes in a boiling water bath.

Makes 3 to 4 quarts.

Garlic Pickled Eggs

Take these along on picnics, pack them in bag lunches, or serve them as an appetizer, sliced and topped with dill mayonnaise. If you use a dark vinegar, roll the eggs in their shells to thoroughly crack them, and don't peel the eggs until ready to use them; they will have a lovely crackled design.

2½ cups champagne or other white wine vinegar; or a dark vinegar, such as red wine or cider, if leaving egg shells on
¾ cup water
½ teaspoon salt
½ teaspoon sugar

9 to 14 hard-boiled eggs (depending on size), peeled or shells cracked in jigsaw pattern
1 teaspoon dried chile flakes
½ teaspoon mustard seed
¼ teaspoon celery seed
4 large garlic cloves, halved

Combine the vinegar, water, salt, and sugar in a medium-sized saucepan over high heat. While the vinegar brine is coming to a boil, pack the hard-boiled eggs and remaining ingredients in a sterilized, still-hot quart jar. Pour the boiling brine over the eggs and spices. Cap immediately with a sterilized, still-hot lid.

Let the jar cool for a couple of hours. Refrigerate for three days before eating.

Makes 1 quart.

Pickled Grape Leaves

Why pay the high price of fancy imported grape leaves in specialty stores when you can pickle your own? Provided you have access to a vine, you can make enough grape leaves to wrap dozens of dolmas. If you don't have a vine or a neighbor with one, look for a vineyard within driving distance. Just after the fall grape harvest (though not just before or during the pick), proprietors are usually more than happy to provide picklers with a few leaves.

> *1 quart water*
> *Whole grape leaves*
> *2 teaspoons salt*
> *1 cup fresh lemon juice or 2½ teaspoons citric acid*
> *1 quart water*

Add the salt to the first quart of water and bring it to a boil. Add the grape leaves for 30 seconds. Drain the leaves and discard the solution.

Form the leaves into loose rolls, and pack them vertically in sterilized, still-hot pint jars.

Add the lemon juice or citric acid to a fresh quart of water. Bring it to a boil, then pour it over the rolls of leaves in jars to cover. If you don't have enough solution, make up more. Wipe rims and cap immediately with still-hot lids, plus rings.

Process the jars in a boiling water bath for 15 minutes.

Sapp Family Dills

In the latter half of the nineteenth century, when my grandparents arrived on Ellis Island from Russia, the immigration authorities found our family name too difficult to pronounce, much less write. So, as for thousands of other immigrants, they took the liberty of giving my grandfather a new name. Unfortunately, no one alive remembers the original name. But we are still making the pickle recipe my grandmother brought with her on the boat—the same one her mother and grandmother and great-grandmother used in their village near Kiev.

4½ pounds firm, fresh pickling cucumbers, each about 2½ inches long
8 large garlic cloves, slightly crushed with the side of a knife
8 dried chile pods
8 slender raw carrots, scraped and sliced lengthwise

2 quarts warm water
8 tablespoons Pickling Spices (see p. 213)
6 tablespoons noniodized salt
1 bunch fresh dill weed (if without seeds, add 2 teaspoons dill seeds)

Soak the cucumbers for 30 minutes in cold water. Wash them well with a vegetable brush, and trim them. Rinse several more times, until no sand remains.

In the bottom of each of four sterilized quart jars, pack the cucumbers vertically. Approximately 5 will fit snugly. Add a garlic clove and chile pod to each. Add another layer of cucumbers; cut some in half, if necessary, to make them fit. Add another garlic clove and chile pod. Pushing hard, put 4 slices of carrot down the sides of each jar, between cucumbers.

In a bowl, mix the warm water with the pickling spices and salt. Stir until the salt dissolves. Pour this solution over the cucumbers, evenly distributing the spices and completely filling the jars. Add dill weed to the top of each jar, curling it into a circle to fit.

Wipe clean the jars and rims, and screw on sterilized caps. Place the jars on a nonreactive surface (nonmetal) on several layers of toweling and let them stand in a warm but not sunny area. The jars may overflow, which means the pickles are processing; change toweling when necessary. If they get low on solution, dissolve 2 ¼ teaspoons salt in 1 cup of warm water and add it to the jars as needed.

Test the dills every few days; they should be well pickled in about a week, depending on the weather. They should still be crispy, not soft and soggy. As soon as they are ready, refrigerate them.

Makes 4 quarts.

Ceviche

Ceviche is traditionally served as a first course or as a side dish to Latin American meals. I also like to heap a large spoonful on top of a plate of fresh salad greens for a quick and savory summer lunch.

½ pound fillets of white fish, such as flounder, bass, or snapper
½ pound baby scallops (or bay, the larger sea scallops, if available)

1¾ cups fresh lime juice
¼ cup fresh lemon juice
1 recipe Three-Chile-Pepper Salsa or Salsa Verde Alameda (see pp. 116, 117).

Cut fish in ¾ inch cubes, reserving juices. Leave baby scallops whole, or halve sea scallops, reserving juices. Put seafood and its juice in a shallow glass or ceramic dish with the lime and lemon juices. Cover and marinate in the refrigerator. After 4 hours, toss to redistribute juices; refrigerate again until scallops and fish turn opaque—4 more hours.

Drain the seafood, again reserving the juices, and toss it with the salsa. Add reserved juices to taste. Put the seafood in salsa back in the pickling container, cover, and refrigerate at least 3 hours before serving.

Makes 1 pound.

Chapter Three

THE VERSATILE CONDIMENT:
CHUTNEY

If it sounds as though I am a chutney lover, so be it.
I plead guilty. To dismiss any condiment as varied
and versatile as chutney as a mere "relish" is
downright wicked in my admittedly prejudiced
opinion.

Betsy Balsey
Food Editor, *Los Angeles Times*

Americans and Canadians and especially the British equate chutney with Major Grey's, that feisty, sweet blend of mangoes, ginger, spices, and vinegar. Contrary to popular assumption, in India people don't eat Major Grey's, nor, largely, are they aware of it. Major Grey's was supposedly developed by an eighteenth-century British officer stationed in India, not an Indian cook.

The sweet and spicy concoctions we call chutneys, Indians refer to as pickles. And what we might call a sauce, or even a dip, an Indian cook will refer to as chutney (literally, as *catni*). In authentic Indian cooking the size of the vegetable and fruit pieces determines whether a condiment is a pickle or a chutney, either of which can be hot and made with vinegar and a good deal of ginger.

But that's India and this is not, which is why, other than Fresh Mint Cress Chutney and Julie Sahni's recipe for Sweet and Sour Tamarind Relish, these are not authentic recipes. While they do utilize lots of produce and enhance a dreary meal, you won't find these chutneys anywhere in India. Instead they follow the traditional North American and English style for chutney—mixing sweet with sour and spicing with such items as garlic, onion, ginger, and chiles. Some recipes require long cooking times, others no cooking at all. A few don't qualify as a Western version of chutney, but as relishes with other types of spicing they slipped into this chapter.

More and more people today keep salt and fat to a minimum in both their cooking and their eating habits. Relishes provide a delicious way to create flavorful dishes without adding sodium, fat, or cholesterol. For less health-conscious individuals, both relishes and chutneys can be used as bases for elaborate, rich sauces, salad dressings, and marinades. Also use chutneys to fill puff pastry hors d'oeuvres, to toss with poultry stuffing, or simply to blend with a little cream cheese for a spread on crispy homemade melba toast. And then, of course, you can serve them with curries, sliced meats, steamed vegetables, and with rice and egg dishes.

Tricolor Pepper and Fennel Relish

A colorful picnic relish, perfect for grilled sausages or hot dogs and beer.

10 cups (4 to 4½ pounds) yellow, green, and red bell peppers, seeded, and diced
6 cups (2 to 2¼ pounds) fennel bulbs, diced
1 cup (about ⅓ pound) yellow onion, diced

1¾ cups sugar
1 tablespoon salt
3¼ cups white distilled vinegar
2 tablespoons mustard seed
2 teaspoons celery seed

Combine the bell peppers, fennel, and onion in a large pot—one that holds at least 4- to 6-quart size. Cover them with boiling water; let them stand 5 minutes, then drain them and discard the liquid. Repeat the boiling water process. Set the vegetables aside.

In the same large pot, bring the sugar, salt, vinegar, and seeds to a boil. Stir in the drained vegetables, reduce the heat, and simmer the mixture about 15 minutes—until it is thickened slightly but the vegetables still retain some crispness.

Ladle the relish into seven sterilized, still-hot pint jars. Wipe rims, and cap immediately with still-hot lids, plus rings. Process 15 minutes in a boiling water bath.

Makes 7 pints.

The Garlic Lover's
Quick Tomato Relish

Need I say more about this recipe than its name? Actually this isn't as garlicky as the name implies. True stinking-rose aficionados will claim I don't use nearly enough, while others will undoubtedly choose to add less than the recommended amount. Follow your own taste. Use this relish to top hamburgers, and other grilled meats, or alongside slices of cold lamb or roast beef.

½ pound tomatoes, seeded and diced
2 green onions, minced
2 garlic cloves, minced
2 teaspoons drained capers, lightly chopped

1 teaspoon virgin olive oil
½ teaspoon minced fresh oregano
⅛ teaspoon freshly ground black pepper

Combine all ingredients in a small bowl. Refrigerate 30 to 60 minutes before serving.

Makes 1 ½ to 2 cups.

Sweet and Sour Tamarind Relish

["IMLI CHUTNEY"]

Tamarind has a lovely tart flavor, just sour enough to pucker the taste buds. This recipe comes from *Classic Indian Cooking*, by noted authority Julie Sahni. She recommends that you serve this rather feisty condiment with potato *samosas* (savory stuffed pastries) or bean dumplings.

1 lemon-sized ball (about ¼ pound) of tamarind, available at international markets
2½ cups boiling water
½ cup unsulphured molasses or packed brown sugar
¼ cup golden raisins
¼ cup diced pitted dates
1½ teaspoons ground toasted cumin seeds (see below)

1 teaspoon Garam Masala *(see p. 218)*
1 teaspoon ground ginger
¼ to ½ teaspoon cayenne pepper
2 teaspoons kosher salt
*1 teaspoon black salt (*kala namak; *optional), available at international markets*

Put the tamarind in a bowl and add 1 cup of the boiling water. Cover and let soak for ½ hour. With the back of a spoon or your fingers, mash it into a thick pulpy sauce. Add the remaining 1½ cups of boiling water, mix well, and let stand. When the pulp is cool enough to handle, mash it again for a minute. Strain the pulp through a sieve or cheesecloth into another bowl, squeezing as much liquid from it as possible. Discard the fibrous residue.

Stir the remaining ingredients into the tamarind liquid. Cover and let rest—at least 4 hours at room temperature, or overnight in the refrigerator—before serving.

This relish keeps well in the refrigerator for about a week. It can also be frozen; defrost thoroughly before serving.

ABOUT TOASTING CUMIN SEEDS

Place cumin seeds in an ungreased skillet. Cook over medium-high heat until seeds begin to darken.

Makes about 3 cups.

Salachat Chatzilim

[ISRAELI EGGPLANT RELISH]

Israelis traditionally eat eggplant dishes such as this one as a salad or side dish. In fact, its Hebrew name means "eggplant salad," although this is so flavorful I like to use it as a relish. Serve it alongside an array of other vegetable dishes or cold, sliced meats, or simply spread it on chunks of homemade bread.

2 medium (2 to 2½ pounds) eggplants

4 medium (about 1 pound) tomatoes, peeled, seeded (see Notes to the Cook), and diced

½ cup minced or grated onion

½ cup minced fresh parsley

1 to 2 garlic cloves, minced

¼ cup virgin olive oil

2 tablespoons fresh lemon or lime juice

1 teaspoon salt

⅛ teaspoon freshly ground black pepper

¼ teaspoon ground cumin

Dash cayenne pepper

Char the eggplants over a hot grill or under a broiler until blackened and wrinkled. Turn the whole eggplants every few minutes until each side chars evenly. Or you may puncture the eggplants in a few spots, place them on a cookie sheet, and bake them in a hot oven (375° to 400°F) for 45 to 60 minutes. Peel the skin, or lightly rub it off under running water. Squeeze the eggplant to release bitter juices.

Chop or mash the eggplant. Combine it with the remaining ingredients in a bowl, and cover. Refrigerate for 1 hour to let flavors combine.

VARIATIONS

There are dozens of ways to make this relish. Some people prefer to toss it with *tahini* instead of oil and lemon. Others add a roasted, peeled, and chopped bell pepper. Still another method calls for frying the mixture in the oil until blackened, and stirring in the lemon juice and seasonings last.

Makes about 5 cups.

Red Onion and Date Relish

Superficially this quick-to-make relish resembles Onion Jam with Grenadine (p. 129). Appearances can be so deceiving! The jam goes best with lighter, more elegant foods, while this sweet and sour relish begs to be served at a picnic, alongside hearty fare. If you're expecting a crowd, you may wish to double or even triple the recipe.

1½ pounds red onions, sliced or roughly chopped
½ cup sugar (if using commercial chopped dates coated in sugar, reduce added sugar to ¼ cup)

½ cup chopped dates
⅓ cup white wine vinegar
⅛ teaspoon ground ginger
¼ teaspoon cayenne pepper

Combine the onions and sugar in a 2- to 3-quart pot over medium-high heat; stir until the sugar melts. Mix in the remaining ingredients and reduce the heat to medium. Simmer, stirring occasionally, until most of the liquid evaporates—about ½ hour. Remove from heat.

Let the relish cool completely. Refrigerate, and serve chilled.

Makes 1½ to 2 cups.

Golden Pear Chutney

Use with curried chicken or with seafood dishes in which the ingredients won't compete with the delicate pear flavor.

3 pounds pears, peeled, cored, and chopped

¼ pound lemons, minced zest and scraped pulp and juice only

1 garlic clove, minced

1¼ cups chopped dried pears

1¼ cups packed light-brown sugar

½ cup light corn syrup

¾ cup white distilled vinegar

½ teaspoon ground ginger

½ teaspoon ground cinnamon

½ teaspoon salt

¼ teaspoon dried chile flakes

¼ teaspoon dry mustard powder

2 tablespoons chopped dried cherries or apricots (optional)

Combine all ingredients in a 3- or 4-quart pot. Bring them to a boil over high heat. Partially cover, reduce heat, and cook at a low, even boil until thick and syrupy—about 1 hour. Stir occasionally to prevent sticking.

Ladle the chutney into three clean pint jars; cap immediately, then refrigerate. Or, for shelf storage, use sterilized jars and lids and process 10 minutes in a boiling water bath.

Makes 3 pints.

Fresh Mint Cress Chutney

I particularly like mint chutney for its extraordinarily refreshing quality. It makes a great accompaniment to grilled lamb, pork chops, or a full-flavored fish. You also might try sprinkling a spoonful over sliced tomatoes, green salad, or steamed vegetables. This recipe makes enough for a crowd. If you're not expecting one, you may wish to halve it; the quality won't change.

2 cups chopped fresh mint leaves
¾ cup chopped watercress leaves
½ cup minced onion
1 tablespoon minced gingerroot
1 tablespoon fresh lemon juice
2 teaspoons minced lemon zest
½ teaspoon minced jalapeño chile pepper
½ teaspoon sugar
¼ teaspoon minced fresh garlic

Combine all ingredients in a medium-sized bowl. Serve immediately or refrigerate, covered, for a few hours until ready to use. Will keep several days refrigerated.

Makes 3 ⅓ cups.

Cranberry Chutney with Tart Green Apple

Great alongside Thanksgiving turkey.

¾ pound fresh cranberries
1½ pounds tart green apples, peeled, cored, and chopped
¼ cup chopped onion
2 teaspoons minced gingerroot
½ cup cider vinegar

½ cup orange juice
1 cup sugar
¼ teaspoon salt
⅛ teaspoon cayenne pepper
1½ cups chopped celery

Combine all ingredients but the celery in a 3-quart pot. Over high heat, bring the mixture to a boil. Reduce the heat to medium and simmer, uncovered, until mixture is thick—15 to 20 minutes. Stir occasionally to prevent sticking. Add the celery and cook 5 more minutes.

Serve while still warm, or cool and ladle into clean jars. Keeps several weeks in the refrigerator.

Makes about 1 quart.

Tamarillo and Green Pepper Chutney

The tamarillo is one of several exotic fruits from New Zealand that are infiltrating American produce markets. My guess is that, though tamarillos are now as unknown as kiwis were several years ago, in a few more years tamarillos will be equally as popular. As people get used to their unusual taste and begin requesting them at markets, tamarillos will become more available. For now, they tend to be a little hard to find, and a bit on the expensive side when you do locate them. Nevertheless, they prove well worth the search.

6 cups water
¾ pound tamarillos
1 pound green bell peppers, seeded and chopped
½ cup chopped onion
2 garlic cloves, minced
¼ cup chopped walnuts
¾ cup packed brown sugar
1 fresh serrano (or other small and hot) chile pepper, minced
1½ teaspoons freshly grated turmeric (or, if unavailable, gingerroot)
½ teaspoon freshly grated nutmeg
1 cup red fruit vinegar

Bring the water to a boil in a large pot. Drop in the tamarillos. Cook them 15 seconds, and pour them into a colander in the sink. Use a knife to slip off the loosened peels. Cut the tamarillos into halves, and puree them in a food processor. Pour the puree through a sieve to remove all seeds; press on the seeds with the back of a broad spoon to squeeze out all puree. Discard seeds. Pour puree into a 2- to 3-quart pot.

Add the remaining ingredients to the puree, and stir to blend the mixture well. Bring it to a boil over high heat, then reduce the heat and cook at a simmer until the mixture is thick—about 1 hour. Stir occasionally to prevent sticking.

Ladle the chutney into one large, clean jar or three half-pint jars. Cap, cool to room temperature, and refrigerate. Keeps one to two weeks.

Makes 3 cups.

Plum and Peach Chutney

This hearty chutney complements any curry dish, no matter how hot, as well as leg of lamb, crown pork roast, and meat stews.

1¾ pounds plums, peeled,
pitted, and chopped
1 pound peaches, peeled,
pitted, and chopped
¾ pound tart apples, peeled,
cored, and chopped
¼ pound yellow onions, peeled
and chopped
¼ pound purple onions, peeled
and chopped

1 cup golden raisins
2 cups cider vinegar
1¼ cups sugar
1½ teaspoons minced fresh
turmeric or gingerroot
½ teaspoon ground allspice
½ teaspoon ground cloves
½ teaspoon ground ginger
1 teaspoon salt
¼ teaspoon cayenne pepper

Combine all ingredients in a 3-quart pot over high heat. When the mixture boils, partially cover it and reduce the heat to medium. Cook until thickened—45 minutes to 1 hour. Stir often to prevent sticking.

Ladle the chutney into three sterilized, still-hot pint jars. Wipe rims and cap immediately with still-hot lids, plus rings. Process 10 minutes in a boiling water bath.

Makes 3 pints.

Fresh Pineapple Chutney
with Macadamias

If you have pineapple mint growing in your garden or know someone who does, it adds a distinctive touch to this chutney. Serve this with pork chops, ham, or pork roast.

3½ cups packed brown sugar
2 tablespoons honey
3 cups white distilled vinegar
1 tablespoon minced fresh gingerroot
1 garlic clove, minced
½ teaspoon salt

⅛ teaspoon freshly ground black pepper
1 4-pound pineapple, peeled and diced, including juice
½ cup chopped macadamia nuts
2 tablespoons minced fresh pineapple mint or other mint

In a 4-quart pot over medium-high heat, bring the sugar, honey, vinegar, gingerroot, garlic, salt, and pepper to a boil. Stir in the pineapple. Partially cover, and let the mixture cook at a low boil for 50 minutes. Add the nuts and mint. Cook uncovered until the chutney thickens—10 to 15 more minutes.

Ladle the chutney into five sterilized still-hot half-pint jars. Wipe rims and cap immediately with still-hot lids, plus rims. Process 10 minutes in a boiling water bath.

Makes 5 cups.

Tomato, Apple, and Currant Chutney

This is probably the most adaptable of all the chutneys in the chapter. Use it to top crackers and yogurt cheese, with grilled meat, or as an ingredient in sauces and dressings—and, of course, with curry dishes.

2½ pounds tomatoes, peeled
   (see Notes to the Cook)
   and coarsely chopped
Juice from 1 tomato, reserved
   while chopping
1½ pounds tart apples,
   peeled, cored, and chopped
½ pound yellow onion, peeled
   and chopped
⅔ cup dried currants

2 cups packed brown sugar
1¼ cups red wine vinegar of
   at least 4 percent acidity
1 tablespoon minced fresh
   gingerroot
1 large garlic clove, minced
½ teaspoon dry mustard
   powder
2 teaspoons salt
½ teaspoon dried chile flakes

Combine all ingredients in a 4-quart pot. Over medium-high heat, bring the mixture to a boil. Reduce the heat to medium, partially cover, and simmer, stirring occasionally, until thick—about 1 hour.

Pour the hot chutney into three sterilized, still-hot pint jars. Wipe rims and cap immediately with still-hot lids, plus rings. Process 15 minutes in a boiling water bath.

Makes 3 pints.

Piquant Papaya and Kiwi Chutney

Not all chutneys require cooking or added sugar or vinegar. This one is just such an exception. You can make it right before serving or prepare it ahead to let the flavors develop, but don't make it too far ahead—it may get hotter than you wish. Of course, if you prefer your chutney extra hot, do let it stand; even throw in the whole chile. The half chile I recommend gives it a medium-hot punch. Serve with bland curry dishes and cold, sliced meats. It goes particularly well with ham.

> *1 medium papaya, ripe but firm*
> *2 kiwis, ripe but firm*
> *½ small, red serrano chile pepper, minced*
> *½ teaspoon minced fresh mint*
> *1 teaspoon fresh lime or lemon juice*

Peel the papaya, remove the seeds, and dice it. (If your papaya is large, you can use the excess and the seeds to make Papaya Seed Dressing, p. 27). Set it aside in a small bowl.

Peel and dice the kiwis, and add them to the papaya. Stir in the minced chile, mint, and lime juice.

Serve immediately or refrigerate a couple of hours.

Makes 1½ to 2 cups.

Green Mango with Dried Fig Chutney

Mango has long been the forerunner among popular chutney fruits. This comes as no surprise; the mango can adapt to just about any recipe, bringing a sweet and almost tangy flavor unrivaled by other fruits. If you are an ardent mango fan and wish to make your chutney pure (without the addition of dried fruit), then do just that. (You may need to reduce the spices; taste before canning.) Serve this alongside slices of roast duck or goose.

1½ cups cider vinegar
3¾ cups sugar
7 cups peeled and coarsely chopped green mangoes (6 or 7 medium)
1¼ cups chopped dried figs

¼ cup minced gingerroot
1 garlic clove, minced
¼ teaspoon dried chile flakes (or more, if a hot chutney is desired)
Dash ground nutmeg

In a 4-quart pot over medium heat, bring the vinegar to a boil. Add the sugar and stir until melted. Add the remaining ingredients. Continue cooking, stirring occasionally and scraping the bottom, until the chutney is thick and the fruit appears translucent—about 45 minutes.

Ladle the chutney into seven sterilized, still-hot half-pint jars. Wipe rims, cap immediately with still-hot lids plus rings, and process 10 minutes in a boiling water bath.

Makes 7 cups.

Chapter Four

SAVORING EVERY BITE: SAUCES, MARINADES, AND PIQUANT PRESERVES

Woe to the cook whose sauces had no sting.

Chaucer

Chaucer, the ancient Persians, and King Sardanapalus of Assyria had something culinary in common. Each passionately loved sauces. Their cooks knew that simple mixtures could work miracles on a tough rabbit, a gamey pheasant, or an old piece of meat. The Persians were the first to discover that a little bit of tart, clabbered cream blended with cooked meat juice made a common dish uncommon. Later, people of the Middle Ages added pastelike mixtures to nearly everything edible; they spread cameline sauce, a raging medieval favorite of toast crumbs, vinegar, and cinnamon, on a variety of meats. Another sauce, Saracen—a blend of almonds, vinegar, and spiced raisins—often accompanied boiled pork.

Sauces became so popular by the eighteenth century that France created sauce-making guilds—masters' unions whose only craft was to make and supply sauces to the public. But Europe wasn't the only continent inventing new ways to serve plain foods. In the New World, the Aztecs and Mayans also were developing tempting concoctions—notably guacamole, that heavenly combination of mashed avocados and pungent spices. Early European explorers became enamored of an unusual Aztec sauce served with pit-grilled meats. The ingredients—chocolate, hot chile peppers, spices, and herbs such as oregano—formed flavors entirely new to Europeans.

While ingredients have changed and occasionally a new method of preparation has been introduced, sauces still play the same role—one that is cultural as well as culinary. People everywhere adore sauces. And they can get quite feisty about their recipes; in the South, for example, sauce makers practically wage war in annual barbecue competitions to determine whether Louisiana or Texas makes a better "Q."

Which sauce do you think is number one today in the United States? If you guessed ketchup, you're right. But it isn't American in origin. In fact, there has been some debate about its genesis. Many food historians, Reay Tannahill among them, think ketchup origi-nated in China, as evidenced by the Siamese word *kachiap*. Tannahill believes Chinese travelers carried it to India, where the English dis-covered it, then took it to England and on to Colonial America. As early as 1814, ketchup appeared in a French cookbook, *L'art du cuisi-nier*, which was written by the gifted chef Beauvilliers as a sampler of fine English cuisine.

Today, with new sauces to sample appearing almost daily in cook-books and on restaurant menus and supermarket shelves, clearly we are a sauce-indulging public. And our love of them, like the sauces themselves, is the product of a long heritage.

Nan Yang Hot Sauce

Philip and Nancy Chu, owners of Nan Yang in Oakland, California, serve this searing Burmese sauce with a number of house specialties, notably pan-fried noodles. I think it is also splendid over their crispy, savory stuffed *samosas*. You might serve it as well with egg rolls.

1 medium tomato, diced
1 garlic clove, minced
¼ fresh red Thai chile pepper
*   or ½ serrano chile pepper,*
*   minced*

1½ tablespoons fresh lemon
*   juice*
1 tablespoon rice vinegar
1 teaspoon sugar
Pinch salt

Combine all ingredients in a small bowl. For a smoother texture, pulse in a food processor just once or twice. The sauce should be quite coarse, not smooth.

Serve immediately, or refrigerate for a couple of hours to let the flavors blend.

Makes ½ cup.

Love Apple Sauce with Aji

"Love apple" was an early name given to the tomato. Where the name came from no one is sure, but it has been around at least since the fifteenth century. Rumors say it was coined when Sir Walter Raleigh presented the fruit as a gift to Queen Elizabeth I. In the Mayan language, *aji* described a vegetable in the pepper family. Serve this sauce over pasta, steamed scallops, or ricotta-filled crepes.

¾ pound tomatoes, peeled, seeded (see Notes to the Cook), and chopped
¼ pound green bell pepper, seeded and chopped
4 green onions, chopped
2 tablespoons chopped fresh dill
2 tablespoons olive oil
1 tablespoon red wine
1 teaspoon crème fraîche *(see p. 135 or 136) or sour cream*
Salt

In a medium skillet, over medium-high heat, combine the vegetables and dill with olive oil and wine. Cook, stirring occasionally, until the vegetables soften—about 10 minutes.

Transfer the mixture to a food processor or blender. Puree until smooth. Return it to the pan; stir in the *crème fraîche* or sour cream. Reheat gently, being careful not to boil.

Makes 1¼ cups.

Old-Fashioned Ketchup

Many malt vinegars do not contain a high enough acidity level for proper canning. Hence, I suggest you refrigerate this ketchup instead, since a more acidic vinegar would alter the flavor.

6 pounds ripe tomatoes,
    chopped
1 small purple onion, peeled
    and chopped
2 teaspoons dried chervil or
    parsley
1½ cups malt vinegar
½ cup plus 2 tablespoons
    packed brown sugar

¾ tablespoon salt
Dash white pepper
1 cinnamon stick, halved
½ nutmeg (tap carefully with
    a hammer)
½ teaspoon mustard seeds
½ teaspoon dried chile flakes
1 teaspoon fennel seeds

Place the tomatoes, onion, and chervil or parsley in a 4- to 5-quart pot. Bring them to a boil over high heat, reduce the heat to medium, and cook until the tomatoes are softened—20 to 25 minutes.

Press the tomato mixture through a fine sieve, pressing hard on the solids with the back of a broad wooden spoon to release the puree. Return the puree to the pot and discard the solids.

Add the vinegar, sugar, salt, and white pepper to the puree. Tie the remaining ingredients in several layers of cheesecloth, and add them to the pot. Bring the mixture to a boil over high heat, reduce the heat to medium, and cook 2 to 2½ hours, uncovered. As it cooks, periodically remove the froth that rises and stir down the sides. When the mixture is very thick, remove the tied spices.

Ladle the ketchup into a jar. Allow it to cool, and refrigerate. Keeps indefinitely.

Makes 2½ cups.

Peach Ketchup

For ages, the Europeans have been making their ketchups out of everything but tomatoes. In fact, tomato ketchup only came about as a result of the colonists' substitutions for unavailable ingredients. Traditionally, ketchups have been made with fruit, mushrooms, and nuts—wonderful ingredients that make superb sauces.

5 pounds ripe peaches, peeled, pitted, and chopped
2½ cups champagne or other white wine vinegar of 5 percent acidity
1 teaspoon salt
1 pound (1 box) brown sugar
1 small vanilla bean
2 2-inch strips orange zest
1 teaspoon mustard seed
1 cinnamon stick
1 ½-inch slice peeled gingerroot
1 teaspoon whole cloves
1 nutmeg, cracked (tap carefully with a hammer)
1 teaspoon juniper berries

Combine the chopped peaches, vinegar, salt, and brown sugar in a 4-quart pot. Tie the remaining ingredients in several layers of cheesecloth and add this to the pot. Over high heat, bring the ingredients to a boil. Reduce the heat to medium, cover, and simmer until the peaches are extremely soft—about 30 minutes.

With a slotted spoon, transfer the peaches to a fine sieve and push them through, or put in a blender or food processor and puree them. Return the pureed peaches to the pot with the cooking liquid and tied spices. Simmer the mixture, uncovered, until quite thick—

about 1 hour. Remove the tied spices and the froth from the top, using a shallow spoon.

Ladle the ketchup into five or six sterilized, still-hot half-pint jars. Wipe rims and cap immediately with still-hot lids, plus rings. Process in a boiling water bath for 15 minutes.

Makes 5 to 6 cups.

Sweet and Tart Cherry Ketchup

Use in place of traditional tomato ketchup or serve as a side sauce to grilled meats and poultry.

2 pounds sweet cherries, stemmed and pitted
1 cup red wine vinegar of at least 5 percent acidity
2 tablespoons sweet red wine or grape juice
½ pound brown sugar
¼ teaspoon salt

¼ teaspoon ground mace
1 teaspoon mustard seed
1 dried chile pod
½ teaspoon green peppercorns
½ teaspoon whole allspice
1 nutmeg, cracked (tap carefully with a hammer)

Combine in a large pot the cherries, vinegar, wine, sugar, salt, and mace. Tie the remaining ingredients in several layers of cheesecloth; add this to the pot, and cover it. Bring the mixture to a boil over high heat, then reduce the heat and simmer until the cherries soften—10 to 15 minutes.

With a slotted spoon, transfer the cherries to a fine sieve and push them through, or to a food processor or blender and puree them. Return the pureed cherries to the pot with the cooking liquid and tied spices. Continue simmering until ketchup thickens—about 1 hour. Remove spices.

Ladle the ketchup into three sterilized, still-hot half-pint jars. Wipe rims and cap immediately with still-hot lids, plus rings, and process 15 minutes in a boiling water bath.

Makes 3 cups.

Spiced Chile Sauce

So much better than store-bought. A great sauce for topping hamburgers, ground lamb burgers, or meat loaf. Make this savory chile sauce in large batches when tomatoes are fresh. Freeze it in pint containers for year-round use.

1 pound fresh tomatoes
1 pound fresh tomatoes,
*   peeled, seeded (see Notes to*
*   the Cook), and coarsely*
*   chopped*
¼ pound onions, chopped
2 fresh jalapeño chile peppers,
*   seeded and minced*
1 small Anaheim chile pepper,
*   chopped*

2 cloves garlic, pushed through
*   a press*
⅓ cup balsamic vinegar
1 teaspoon fresh lemon juice
2 tablespoons packed brown
*   sugar*
1 teaspoon salt
¼ teaspoon ground allspice
Dash ground cloves

Puree the first batch of tomatoes with the peels on in a food processor. Press the puree through a sieve with the back of a broad spoon until only seeds and peel solids are left, and discard these.

In a 3- or 4-quart large pot, combine the tomato puree with the chopped tomatoes and remaining ingredients, and stir well. Over high heat, bring tomato mixture to a boil. Reduce the heat, and simmer, stirring occasionally, until thick—about 1 hour. Allow the sauce to cool, ladle it into containers, and refrigerate or freeze.

Makes 1 ¾ cups.

Olallieberry Barbecue Sauce

I'll challenge "Q" sauces in Louisiana or Texas any day with this recipe. The berries give it an unusual, distinctive flavor, yet the sauce maintains good old barbecue taste.

1 pound tomatoes, peeled (see Notes to the Cook)
1 cup olallieberries (or if unavailable, boysenberries)
2 tablespoons Worcestershire sauce
1 teaspoon Liquid Smoke
2 teaspoons Dijon mustard
¼ pound red onion, minced
2 large garlic cloves, minced
1½ tablespoons packed brown sugar
2 tablespoons red berry vinegar
½ teaspoon dried chile flakes
¼ teaspoon salt
¼ teaspoon ground cumin

Puree the tomatoes and berries in a processor. Pour the puree through a fine sieve into a medium-sized saucepan. Press hard with the back of a broad spoon to release all the puree. Discard the solids. Stir in the remaining ingredients, and bring the mixture to a boil. Reduce the heat, and simmer until thick—30 to 35 minutes. The sauce should be reduced by half. Use immediately, or, when cool, refrigerate.

Makes 1½ cups.

Matthew and Jeffrey's Favorite Barbecue Sauce

Some people can get eighteen things accomplished in the same time it takes you and me to do one. Matthew and Jeffrey's mother, Irene Muzio, is one of those people. And she never skimps on quality, particularly when it comes to cooking. Her husband, Jay, and two young sons have learned to expect great and wonderful things from her, like this easy, last-minute sauce. Use it to baste chicken, pork, or ribs while you bake or grill them. Pass the remaining sauce in a small bowl.

½ cup peach or nectarine jam
½ cup ketchup
1 tablespoon red fruit vinegar
1 garlic clove, pushed through a press

½ teaspoon Worcestershire sauce
½ teaspoon grated gingerroot

In a medium-sized saucepan, over medium heat, melt the jam for about 2 minutes. Stir in the remaining ingredients. Heat, stirring occasionally, until the sauce is quite warm. Use immediately.

Makes a little more than 1 cup.

Gingered Tomato Coulis

A *coulis* is traditionally a gravy, but modern formulations give it a wider range of usage and ingredients. This chunky, mild version hints of onion, garlic, and ginger. Serve it with cold, sliced meats and a glass of hearty red wine to cool a warm summer night.

2 tablespoons olive oil	1 green onion, minced
1 tablespoon safflower or vegetable oil	2 ½ pounds ripe tomatoes, peeled, seeded (see Notes to the Cook), and chopped
1 teaspoon grated gingerroot	
1 small red onion, minced	Salt
1 garlic clove, minced	Pinch white pepper

In a large saucepan, over a medium-high flame, heat the oils. Add the ginger, onion, garlic, and green onion. Sauté them 3 to 4 minutes—until the onion is translucent. Add the chopped tomatoes, and stir to combine well. Reduce the heat, and simmer until very thick and saucelike—25 to 35 minutes. Stir frequently to prevent mixture from sticking to the pan. Season with salt to taste and pepper.

Cool the *coulis* to room temperature. Refrigerate at least 3 hours before serving.

Makes two cups.

Skordalia

[GREEK GARLIC SAUCE]

The Greeks have given the world so much: mythology, culture, history, and *skordalia*—in my mind, one of the most sumptuous of sauces. Strong flavors often add sensuousness to a meal, and *skordalia*'s are far from the exception. For an unusual appetizer, prepare a bowl of *skordalia* with a platter of fried eggplant and zucchini sticks.

1¼ pounds potatoes, well scrubbed
1 large egg yolk
2 tablespoons herb vinegar
3 tablespoons fresh lemon juice
4 large garlic cloves, pushed through a press
1 teaspoon salt
Pinch cayenne pepper
½ cup virgin olive oil
2 anchovies

Puncture each potato with a fork, and bake them 1 hour in a 400°F oven. Cool, and remove skins.

In a food processor, pulse the potatoes until they are thoroughly mashed. Add the egg yolk, vinegar, lemon juice, garlic, salt, and cayenne. Blend until very smooth—about 1 minute. With the machine running, gradually add the oil.

Transfer the *skordalia* to a bowl, and garnish it with whole anchovies.

Makes 2 cups.

Pancetta Sauce

Use to top omelettes, pasta, and sautéed veal medallions.

⅓ cup thinly sliced pancetta, *chopped*
1 small yellow onion, peeled and minced
2 garlic cloves, minced
3 tablespoons olive oil

4 teaspoons tomato paste
3 tablespoons red wine
1 tablespoon crème fraîche *(see p. 135 or 136) or sour cream*

In a small skillet, sauté the *pancetta*, onion, and garlic in olive oil over medium-high heat. Cook until the *pancetta* turns light pink—about 3 minutes. Stir in the tomato paste thoroughly. Add the red wine, reduce the heat to low, and cook, stirring, 2 minutes. Stir in the *crème fraîche*.

Serve the sauce immediately.

Makes ¾ cup.

Thyme-Flavored Mustard Sauce

A strong and assertive condiment, mustard sauce goes best with meats that can stand up to it, such as roast beef or grilled lamb. Avoid using with fish; the mustard and vinegar overwhelm delicate seafood flavors.

½ cup Dijon mustard
¼ cup safflower oil
2 tablespoons heavy cream (or if unavailable, half-and-half)

1 teaspoon white wine vinegar
1 teaspoon packed brown sugar
1 teaspoon minced fresh thyme
1 teaspoon drained capers
1 shallot, peeled and minced

In a small bowl, whisk together the mustard, oil, cream, and vinegar. Stir in the sugar until lumps disappear. Add the thyme, capers, and shallot.

Serve immediately, or store in the refrigerator until ready to use. Bring to room temperature before serving.

Makes ¾ cup.

Robust Wine Sauce

An excellent sauce over roast beef, sautéed lamb chops, or grilled steaks.

1 cup red wine
3/4 cup lamb stock or beef stock
1/3 cup chopped shallots
1/4 cup coarsely chopped parsley
2 mushrooms, quartered
1 celery stalk, chopped
1 bay leaf

1 tablespoon unsalted butter
1/2 teaspoon dried oregano
1/2 teaspoon dried tarragon
1 tablespoon arrowroot
Salt
Freshly ground black pepper

Combine all ingredients, except the arrowroot and salt and pepper, in a medium-sized saucepan. Over high heat, bring them to a boil and cook 2 minutes. Reduce the heat and simmer 15 minutes. Strain the sauce. Discard solids, and return the liquid to the saucepan.

Sprinkle the arrowroot into a small cup. Stir in 1 teaspoon of the sauce to make a paste. Continue adding 1 teaspoon at a time until the arrowroot mixture becomes quite liquid. Whisk it into the sauce. Over medium heat, simmer the sauce, stirring occasionally, until thickened. Season with salt and pepper to taste.

Serve the sauce immediately.

VARIATION

You may alter the proportions of red wine and stock according to your preference.

Makes 1 to 1 1/4 cups.

Blueberry Amontillado Sauce for Game

Although I don't usually advocate using canned fruits or vegetables, this recipe is an exception. Fresh blueberries just don't create the same result. Also, the canned berries allow you to make this sauce all year around. Think of it especially in the autumn and winter months, when menus more frequently include such game as duck, Cornish game hens, goose, or turkey.

Blueberries from 1 (15-ounce) can, with juice or syrup	*1 vanilla bean*
1½ cups dry amontillado or dry port	*¼ teaspoon whole cloves*
	⅓ cup chicken stock
1 tablespoon minced orange zest	*2 tablespoons blueberry or black currant jelly*
1 small stick cinnamon	*1 tablespoon unsalted butter*
	1 tablespoon arrowroot

Strain the berries and reserve ½ cup of the juice. Set these aside.

Over high heat, in a medium-sized saucepan, bring the sherry to a boil. Tie the orange zest and spices in several layers of cheesecloth, and add them to the sherry. Reduce the heat to medium-high, and cook, reducing the sherry by half. Discard the tied spices.

Over medium heat, stir in the chicken stock, jelly, and the reserved blueberry juice or syrup. Cook 5 minutes. Add the butter and simmer until it is completely melted.

Sprinkle the arrowroot into a small cup. Stir in 1 teaspoon of the hot sauce to make a paste. Continue stirring in 1 teaspoon at a time until the arrowroot mixture becomes liquid. Whisk it into the sauce and cook the sauce over medium- to medium-high heat, stirring occasionally until thickened. Add the strained blueberries.

Serve the sauce immediately.

Makes 1⅔ cups.

Red Bell Pepper with Rosemary Sauce for Pasta

Pasta sauces have come a long way. In medieval Italy, people sauced their pasta with heavy, sweet concoctions of honey and fruit. The colorful savory sauce made by this recipe complements pasta beautifully. For a spectacular dish, serve it with spinach pasta and a topping of roasted, slivered yellow peppers.

2 tablespoons unsalted butter
2 tablespoons olive oil
1 pound red bell peppers, seeded, and chopped
¼ pound yellow onions, chopped
2 garlic cloves, chopped

2 tablespoons prosciutto or coppa, chopped
½ teaspoon minced fresh rosemary or ¼ teaspoon dried rosemary
½ cup half-and-half
Salt
Freshly ground black pepper

Melt the butter with the olive oil in a medium-sized saucepan. Turn up heat to high; add the peppers and onion. Cook them till soft, stirring frequently. Stir in the garlic, prosciutto, and rosemary. Turn heat down to medium; mix in the half-and-half. Cook until thickened slightly—5 to 7 minutes.

Transfer the mixture to a food processor or blender. Process it to a puree in which small flecks of red still appear.

Pour the sauce back into the saucepan and reheat it just slightly. Add salt and pepper to taste. Serve immediately over steaming hot pasta.

Makes about 2¼ cups.

Irish Whiskey Cream Sauce

Before you pass judgment on this recipe's unusual combination of ingredients, give it a devil-may-care try. Irish whiskey and coffee go together marvelously in Irish coffee; why not in sauce? Use your own imagination as to what to serve it with; I like mine over steak, instead of béarnaise.

1 tablespoon unsalted butter
1½ cups chicken stock
2 teaspoons white flour, sifted
½ cup heavy cream
1 tablespoon whole roasted coffee beans

2 teaspoons Irish whiskey
Salt
Freshly ground green peppercorns

Combine the butter and stock in a medium saucepan over high heat. When the butter has melted and the stock boils, whisk in the sifted flour. Add the cream and coffee beans. Over medium-high heat, reduce the mixture to a thick consistency. Stir frequently to prevent sticking to the sides and bottom of the saucepan.

Using a slotted spoon, remove the beans. Stir in the Irish whiskey, and add the salt and ground green peppercorns to taste.

Makes ¾ cup.

Vermouth Hollandaise

Serve over steamed asparagus, broccoli, cauliflower, or a mélange of vegetables.

4 large egg yolks
3 tablespoons dry vermouth
1 tablespoon fresh lemon juice
9 tablespoons chilled unsalted butter

Dash cayenne pepper
Salt
Freshly ground black pepper

Put ½ cup of warm water in the bottom of a double boiler. In the top section, whisk together the egg yolks, vermouth, and lemon juice. Turn up heat to medium—no higher—and whisk in butter, 1 tablespoon at a time. Whisk continuously, and add the next tablespoon of chilled butter as soon as the one before has melted. This prevents the mixture from getting too hot and curdling. If it does start to curdle, quickly remove it from the heat and add 1 to 2 teaspoons of chilled water to cool it before adding more butter.

When all the butter has been added, remove the sauce from the heat. Stir in the cayenne and add salt and pepper to taste. Serve immediately.

Even if the water is too late to smooth the sauce, don't throw it out. Finish whisking in the butter, then smooth the curdled sauce in a food processor or blender. It won't be a finely emulsified sauce, but it won't be a disaster, either.

Makes ¾ to 1 cup.

Tangerine Maltaise Sauce

I know of no more wonderful way to enjoy tender stalks of spring asparagus than with a healthy dollop of *maltaise*.

3 large egg yolks
3 tablespoons fresh tangerine juice
7 tablespoons chilled unsalted butter

2 teaspoons minced tangerine zest
¼ teaspoon sugar
Salt
Freshly ground black pepper

Put ½ cup of warm water in the bottom of a double boiler. In the top section, whisk together the egg yolks and tangerine juice. Turn up heat to medium. Whisk in chilled butter 1 tablespoon at a time. Whisk continuously; as each tablespoon melts and blends with the sauce, immediately whisk in the next. The chilled butter prevents the mixture from getting too hot and curdling. If it does start to curdle, quickly remove it from the heat and add 1 to 2 teaspoons of chilled water to cool it before adding more butter.

When all the butter has been added, remove the sauce from the heat. Stir in the zest and sugar and add the salt and pepper to taste. Serve immediately.

If the mixture does curdle, don't throw it out. Finish whisking in the butter and transfer the mixture to a blender or food processor. Give it a good whirl. If it's not a finely emulsified sauce, neither will it be a waste.

Makes about ⅔ cup.

Rouille

No fish stew or bouillabaisse is worth the cost of its ingredients without a little zesty *rouille*. I suggest making this classic southern French sauce with fresh pimentos; even if it takes a laborious search to find them, they make that much difference. But they can be difficult to locate, so if they elude you, substitute red bell peppers. Bells will make a nice, mild sauce, perfectly acceptable but a little different in flavor from that made with the stronger pimentos.

¾ pound fresh pimentos
½ cup fresh bread cubes
½ cup fish stock
(approximately)
3 medium garlic cloves
1 tablespoon virgin olive oil

2 teaspoons minced, packed
fresh basil
½ teaspoon dried chile flakes
Salt
Freshly ground black pepper

Roast or broil the pimentos until the skin shrivels and chars. Enclose them in a paper bag for 10 minutes to further loosen the skin. Peel the skin, scoop out the seeds and veins, and trim the stems from the tops. Transfer the pimentos to a blender or food processor.

Soak the bread cubes in just enough fish stock to moisten but not saturate them—about ¼ cup. Add them to the blender or food processor along with the garlic, oil, basil, and chile flakes.

With the machine running, add 1 tablespoon at a time of the remaining fish stock until the sauce reaches the desired consistency. Scrape down the sides frequently. About 3 tablespoons of stock will give a hollandaise-like thickness. When the sauce is finished, not before, add salt and pepper to taste.

Makes about 1 cup.

Sauce Basilic

Opposite serene Lake Merritt in Oakland, California, sits La Brasserie, a French restaurant owned by Roger and Kimala Martin. Their daughter, Chantal, came up with the idea for this silky, basil-laden sauce. Kimala, the restaurant's chef, perfected it. Customers came to request it so often that the Martins finally added it to their permanent menu. Serve the sauce over filet mignon, chicken, or fish sautéed in a small amount of oil.

Trace of fat or oil left in skillet from sautéeing meat, chicken, or fish
1 tablespoon chopped shallots
¼ cup dry sherry
¼ cup beef stock
½ cup firmly packed, minced fresh basil leaves

2 medium tomatoes, peeled, seeded (see Notes to the Cook), and diced
1 cup heavy cream
Salt
White pepper

Turn up the heat to medium-high under the skillet with the reserved fat; add the shallots, sherry, and beef stock. Bring the mixture to a boil and reduce it by half.

Turn down the heat to medium; add the basil, tomatoes, and heavy cream. Simmer, stirring occasionally, until the sauce reduces by one-third and thickens—10 to 15 minutes. Remove it from the heat and add salt and pepper to taste.

Serve the sauce immediately.

Makes about 1¼ cups.

Green and Pink Peppercorn Sauce

Serve over a meat that will complement the sauce's full flavors. You might try it with sautéed filet mignon or lamb chops, or grilled flank steak.

2 tablespoons unsalted butter or bacon fat
2 tablespoons flour
1¾ cups beef or veal stock
¼ cup heavy cream
1 tablespoon red wine

1 tablespoon sherry vinegar or red wine vinegar
1 tablespoon green peppercorns
1 tablespoon pink peppercorns
Salt (omit if using bacon fat)

For the basis of the sauce, make a roux: melt the butter or fat in a medium-sized saucepan, over medium-high heat, and stir in the flour. Continue to cook and stir until the roux turns light brown. Whisk in the stock. Bring it to a boil and whisk in the remaining ingredients.

Bring the mixture to a second boil, partially cover, and cook until it is reduced to a thick consistency—15 to 20 minutes.

Serve the sauce immediately.

Makes 1 to 1¼ cups.

Caper and Lemon Butter Sauce

My sister, Jordana, can't get enough capers. In fact, I suspect she puts them on her cornflakes in the morning. Come evening, she can inevitably be found stirring a few into a butter sauce destined for grilled chicken breasts or a fillet of sole.

¼ cup unsalted butter
2 teaspoons fresh lemon juice
½ teaspoon lemon zest,
*   minced*

1 garlic clove, pushed through
*   a press*
3 tablespoons drained capers
Freshly ground black pepper

In a medium-sized skillet, over medium heat, slowly melt the butter. Stir in the lemon juice, zest, and garlic. Add the capers; add pepper to taste. Heat a little while longer—just until hot.

Serve the sauce immediately.

Makes about ⅓ cup.

Three-Chile-Pepper Salsa

Mexican cooks add salsa to a variety of dishes. You might use it particularly to top omelettes, scrambled eggs, or frittata.

This is a fairly hot salsa. If you like yours a little milder, reduce the amount of each chile. Do not omit any chile entirely, or the flavor of the salsa will change. Remember to use rubber gloves when you chop the peppers, or the juices will burn your fingers.

1 pound fresh tomatillos, husks removed

1 pound tomatoes, peeled, seeded (see Notes to the Cook), and quartered

1 fresh red jalapeño chile pepper, minced

1 fresh green Anaheim chile pepper, chopped

2 fresh serrano chile peppers, minced

2 garlic cloves, minced

⅓ pound yellow onion, chopped

2 tablespoons minced fresh cilantro (also called fresh coriander)

1 tablespoon virgin olive oil

½ teaspoon salt

Place the tomatillos in a 1-quart saucepan. Cover them with water; bring them to a boil. Reduce the heat to a simmer and cook the tomatillos until they soften—15 to 20 minutes. Be careful not to cook them so much that the peels break. Transfer the tomatillos to a food processor and pulse only until chopped coarsely—two or three times. Pour the tomatillos into a large mixing bowl.

Also coarsely chop in the food processor six tomato quarters at a time. Add each chopped batch to the tomatillos in the mixing bowl.

Stir in remaining ingredients, cover, and refrigerate at least 6 hours to blend the flavors.

Makes 1 quart.

Salsa Verde Alameda

If you like your salsa hot, don't discard the chile seeds. This salsa will keep for several days, if covered in the refrigerator. Just remember, if you add those seeds, that the longer you keep the salsa the hotter it gets.

For tortilla chips a hundred times better than those packaged, start with fresh corn tortillas. Cut them into pie-shaped wedges. Fry the pieces in hot corn oil, then serve them with your day-old salsa.

2 fresh Anaheim chile peppers
½ pound tomatillos, husks removed
2 fresh small, yellow wax chile peppers, minced (seeds optional)
¼ cup minced fresh cilantro (also called fresh coriander)
1 elephant garlic clove (or two small garlic cloves), minced
¼ pound onions, chopped
2 tablespoons virgin olive oil
2 teaspoons herb vinegar
½ teaspoon salt

Broil the Anaheim chiles until charred on all sides. Immediately enclose them in a paper bag to further loosen the skin. When the chiles are cool, peel, seed, and chop them. Transfer them to a medium-sized bowl.

Add the tomatillos to a large saucepan of water. Bring it to a boil and cook the tomatillos until soft—15 to 20 minutes. Drain them, and mash them in a small bowl with a potato masher. Add them to the Anaheim chiles.

Stir the remaining ingredients into the tomatillo and chile mixture. Cover the salsa and refrigerate it at least 6 hours before serving. This salsa is better the second day.

Makes 1 pint.

Basil Pesto

There is much debate as to whether pesto should be smooth or coarse. Each version has its merits, so follow your instinct. If you want a chunkier pesto, don't use the processor; hand chop the ingredients, then blend them in a bowl. Toss with steaming pasta.

2 garlic cloves, mashed with the side of a knife
2 cups stemmed fresh basil
1 tablespoon pine nuts or walnuts, toasted (see below)

3 tablespoons grated Parmesan or Romano cheese
⅓ cup virgin olive oil
Salt

Place the garlic, basil, nuts, and cheese in a food processor or blender. Turn on the machine; gradually drizzle in the oil. When all the oil has been incorporated, add salt to taste.

Will keep several days refrigerated.

ABOUT TOASTING NUTS

Nuts can be toasted either in a small toaster oven at low heat or pan fried in a greaseless skillet over medium heat until browned on all sides.

Makes about ¾ to 1 cup.

Cilantro Pesto

An unconventional condiment like this pesto made with cilantro can be used to create whole new dishes, when you match its particular flavors with other ingredients. Or you can use it conventionally, such as with hot pasta or stuffed into ripe cherry tomatoes as an appetizer.

1½ cups packed fresh cilantro (also called fresh coriander) leaves
½ cup broken pistachio nut meats
1 medium garlic clove
3 to 4 tablespoons virgin olive oil
¼ cup crumbled feta cheese

Place the cilantro leaves, pistachios, and garlic in a food processor. Pulse just until roughly chopped.

Transfer the mixture to a bowl. Stir in the oil, a tablespoon at a time, until the mixture forms a paste. Mix in the crumbled cheese. Don't overmix; small chunks of cheese should be visible.

Will keep several days refrigerated.

Makes about 1¼ cups.

Chive Pesto with Asiago and Toasted Pumpkin Seeds

For a particularly flavorful, unusual starter course, make a savory *torta*. Soften ½ pound each of unsalted butter and cream cheese. Blend them well. Spoon one-third of the butter mixture into the bottom of a bowl, and spread it with one-half the pesto. Add another one-third of the butter mixture, and spread it with the remaining pesto. Top the *torta* with the last of the butter mixture. Let it sit in the refrigerator for several hours to harden. Turn out the *torta* onto a platter. (Do this by dipping the bowl in a larger bowl of hot water only long enough to loosen the *torta* without melting it—about 5 seconds.) Let the *torta* rest on the platter for several hours before serving it with crackers or baguette slices.

2 cups fresh chopped chives, including a few garlic chives, if available
1 cup stemmed fresh parsley
¾ cup hulled pumpkin seeds, toasted (see below)
2 medium garlic cloves
¾ cup grated Asiago or Romano cheese
5 tablespoons virgin olive oil

Combine the chives, parsley, pumpkin seeds, and garlic in a food processor. Pulse only until roughly chopped.

Transfer the mixture to a bowl. Stir in the cheese and oil by hand. The consistency should be pastelike.

Will keep several days refrigerated.

ABOUT TOASTING PUMPKIN SEEDS

Toast pumpkin seeds either in a toaster oven or pan fry in a greaseless skillet over medium heat until browned on all sides.

Makes 2 cups.

Ginger Marinade for Fish

Use to marinate firm-textured fish, such as halibut or shark. In summer, instead of making kabobs of beef, I marinate chunks of fish to skewer with fresh vegetables for the grill.

4 teaspoons fresh lime juice	1 teaspoon sesame oil
2 teaspoons soy sauce	¼ teaspoon salt (optional)
2 teaspoons grated gingerroot	⅛ teaspoon freshly ground black pepper

Combine the ingredients in a small bowl. Pour them over fish in a shallow baking pan, and marinate at least 1 hour.

Skewer and grill the fish, or bake fillets in a 350°F oven until fish flakes. Serve with additional lime slices.

Makes enough for ½ to 1 pound of fish.

Hecht Poultry Marinade
for the Barbecue

Alma Hecht loves cooking, but she adores barbecuing. Just to hear the subject raised in discussion makes her eyes light like sparks from charcoal and her curls of flaming red hair dazzle with blinding sheen. During one such barbecue discussion she told me about this wonderful apricot and citrus marinade for chicken.

4 tablespoons apricot preserves
2 medium garlic cloves, minced
1 shallot, minced
¼ cup fresh lemon juice
¼ cup fresh orange juice
1 teaspoon fresh thyme or ½ teaspoon dried thyme

1 teaspoon minced, dried orange zest
Salt
Freshly ground black pepper
½ cup white wine
1 tablespoon white wine vinegar

Heat the preserves with the garlic, shallot, and juices in a small saucepan until combined. Add the thyme, orange zest, salt, and pepper to taste. Pour the marinade over poultry.

Bake the poultry for 15 to 20 minutes at 350°F, basting frequently. Remove it from the oven. Degrease the pan, and deglaze it with the white wine and vinegar. Transfer the deglazed marinade to a small saucepan, and reduce it over medium-high heat to a syrupy consistency.

Use the marinade to baste the poultry as you finish cooking it on the barbecue.

Makes enough for 1 chicken or 2 Cornish game hens.

Pineapple Orange Marinade for Ribs

Ribs don't have to be barbecued with smoky sauces. Tangy fruit marinades add an unconventional, slightly sweet flavor.

⅔ cup pineapple juice
2 tablespoons orange juice
2 tablespoons soy sauce
2 tablespoons packed brown
* sugar*

1 tablespoon lime juice
2 teaspoons minced candied
* ginger*
1 tablespoon cornstarch, sifted

Combine all ingredients except the cornstarch in a medium-sized saucepan. Over high heat, bring the mixture to a boil. Reduce the heat to medium.

Put the cornstarch in a small bowl. Mix in a teaspoonful of hot marinade, and stir to make a paste. Continue adding teaspoonfuls, one at a time, until the paste is as liquid as the marinade. Stir the cornstarch mixture into the marinade and, still over medium heat, reheat it to a boil. Let it boil just until marinade thickens—30 to 60 seconds.

When the marinade is cool, pour it over ribs (or other meat). Marinate them in the refrigerator for at least 2 hours.

Bake or grill the ribs as desired. Just before they finish cooking, brush on a final layer of marinade.

Makes about 1 cup. Enough for 2 to 3 pounds of ribs or 1 small chicken.

Herbed Wine Marinade for Poultry and Seafood

If pinched for time, begin marinating the night before. Never mind if the oil congeals. Take marinated items out of refrigerator half an hour before ready to cook.

¼ cup virgin olive oil
½ cup white wine
3 tablespoons minced fresh basil

2 tablespoons white wine vinegar
1 teaspoon minced fresh rosemary
1 large garlic clove, pushed through a press

Mix all the ingredients in a small bowl. Let the marinade sit for 20 minutes to combine the flavors.

In a shallow bowl, pour the marinade over fish fillets, shellfish, or chicken. Turn it to coat all sides. Let it marinate in the refrigerator 3 hours.

During grilling or baking, baste the poultry or seafood.

Makes 1 cup. Enough for 1 small chicken or duck or 3 to 4 fillets of fish.

Spicy Vietnamese Marinade

Nuoc Mam, this recipe's main ingredient, can be found in most Asian food stores. In Thai markets you will find it under the name *Nam Pla*. There really is no acceptable alternative to this clear, fermented fish sauce. This marinade works best with grilled beef or poultry.

⅓ cup Nuoc Mam *or* Nam Pla *(fermented fish sauce)*
3 tablespoons rice vinegar
3 tablespoons fresh lemon juice
1 teaspoon peanut oil
2 tablespoons packed brown sugar

1 tablespoon minced onion
2 garlic cloves, minced
1 fresh serrano chile pepper, minced
2 teaspoons minced fresh cilantro (also called fresh coriander)

About 3 hours before barbecuing, combine all the ingredients in a small bowl. Let the marinade sit for 30 minutes so the flavors can develop. Strain it and discard the solids.

Pour the marinade over poultry or beef and refrigerate. On the grill, baste with the marinade. Pass any remainder in a sauce boat.

Makes ¾ cup. Enough to marinate ½ to 1 pound of beef or poultry slices.

Sage Jelly

For slices of roast turkey, chicken, or duck, this unusual herb jelly makes a marvelous accompaniment. You might try making it instead with rosemary or basil—almost any herb infuses a delicious flavor. If you'd like to brighten its pale yellow hue, add one or two drops of green food coloring.

3 ½ tablespoons chopped fresh
    sage (including stems)
2 cups water
¼ cup fresh lemon juice

¼ teaspoon peanut oil
1 (2-ounce) package powdered
    pectin
3 ½ cups sugar

Combine the sage and water in a small saucepan, and bring them to a boil. Remove from heat. Let the sage steep in the water for 45 minutes. Pour the sage water through a cheesecloth-lined sieve into a 2-quart pot. Discard the sage.

Add to the sage water the lemon juice, oil, and powdered pectin. Whisk briskly until the pectin thoroughly dissolves.

Over high heat, bring the mixture to a boil, stirring continually. Quickly stir in the sugar, and bring the mixture to a second boil. Continue to stir while it boils for 2 minutes. Immediately remove from heat.

Ladle the jelly into four sterilized, still-hot half-pint jars. Wipe rims and cap with still-hot lids, plus rings. Process in a boiling water bath for 10 minutes. Let the jars cool.

Store jars on a cool, dry shelf.

Makes 4 cups.

Calvados Jelly

If you like wine jellies, you'll adore Calvados Jelly. Depending on your taste, it can be a little strong—oh, but how that strength can fortify you on a cold day alongside roast beef, sautéed veal, or grilled lamb. As a cost saver, you may substitute American applejack for the more expensive French calvados. You don't have to seal with paraffin, but it does ensure better and longer preservation.

1 (2-ounce) package powdered pectin
3 cups calvados (apple brandy)
1 tablespoon fresh lemon juice
¼ teaspoon oil
4¼ cups sugar

In a 4-quart pot, mix together the pectin, calvados, lemon juice, and oil. Over high heat, bring the mixture to a full boil. Stir in the sugar. Bring the mixture to a second full, rolling boil. Keep stirring; boil hard 1 minute. Immediately remove the jelly from the heat.

Ladle the jelly into five sterilized, still-hot half-pint jars. You may seal them with paraffin plus lids and rings or with lids and rings alone. Leave ¼ inch headspace if you plan to seal them with paraffin; leave ⅛ inch headspace if not.

To use paraffin, simply melt it and pour a very thin, but uniform layer over the jelly. Add lids and rings to seal. To seal with only lids and rings, put these on the jelly jars immediately after filling. Turn the jars upside down for 3 minutes. Turn right side up again. The lids should seal. Those that do may be stored on a cool, dry shelf. Any that don't seal require refrigeration after cooling.

Makes 5 cups.

Onion Jam with Grenadine

This savory jam is a specialty of the Ardennes region of Belgium. Its popularity in the United States can be attributed to world-famous chef Michel Guerard. Try it with turkey for a memorable Thanksgiving.

5½ tablespoons unsalted butter
1 pound red, sweet onions, chopped
⅓ cup plus 1 tablespoon sugar
½ teaspoon salt
¼ teaspoon white pepper
⅓ cup dried pears, minced
¾ cup red wine
¼ cup red berry vinegar
2 tablespoons grenadine syrup

In a large skillet over medium heat, melt the butter. Add the onions, sugar, salt, and pepper, stirring to combine them well. Cover, reduce heat, and simmer 30 minutes, stirring occasionally.

While the onions cook, soak the minced pears in red wine.

When the onions are quite soft, stir in the pears, wine, vinegar, and grenadine syrup. Over high heat, bring the mixture to a boil, then reduce the heat to medium and cook, uncovered, until thick—20 to 30 minutes. Ladle the jam into two clean, hot half-pint jars. Cap immediately.

Refrigerate when cool. Keeps 1 to 2 months refrigerated.

Makes 2 cups.

Chapter Five

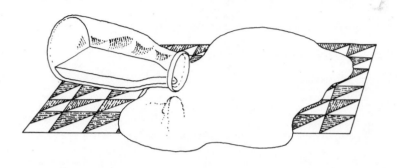

A FINE CAUDLE: DAIRY PRODUCTS

Take a Pint of Milk, turn it with Sack; then strain it,
and when 'tis cold, put it in a Skillet, with Mace,
Nutmeg, and some white bread sliced; let all these
boil, and then beat the Yolks of four or five eggs,
the Whites of two, and thicken your Caudle,
stirring it all one Way for fear it curdle; let it warm
together, then take it off, and Sweeten it to your
Taste.

Mrs. E. Smith
The Compleat Housewife (1736)

There was a time when the city dweller, dependent on commercial food supplies, was an anomaly. On farms, families raised nearly everything they needed and what they couldn't produce themselves they often bartered for, with other farmers or craftsmen. Milk came fresh and raw from the cow each morning, and to store it, in the time before refrigerators, they chilled it however they could.

One of my grandmothers grew up on a farm in central Texas. She remembers well how each morning she or one of the other children walked down to the tree-shaded stream running near the house and drew pails and jugs of milk, cream, butter, and cheese out of the cool, rushing water.

Nana has often described her other chores, such as churning. The first time I heard the story of how she daily pushed on the wooden churn, I imagined it taking the better part of the day. But no, she assured me. When a household has nine children and several adults to share in the chore, the butter separates quickly from the cream.

Although she admits refrigerators are a tremendous convenience, the advent of its predecessor, the icebox, impressed the family even more. No longer would they have to carry heavy pails up from the creek, trudging through mud and rain during the wind-swept winters. From then on, all they had to worry about was mopping up the melted ice water from under the icebox. The ice man did all the hard work; every day he delivered a huge block of ice and inserted it into the icebox my great-great-grandmother had sitting in the very center of the kitchen for all the world to admire.

Nana remembers her years on the farm as full of hard work and long hours. But she also recalls the grander benefits, such as rich, fresh cream so thick they used to spread it like butter with a knife. Now, at ninety, sometimes she drifts into a pleasant reverie and thinks of the better times, when as a young child she used to wake up to the sound of the rooster and at night listen to the crickets telling wild stories. Every now and then, she licks her narrow lips and smiles, crinkling the corners of her dark-brown eyes. "Sure do miss that sweet cream," she says. "There was nothing better."

I don't doubt it. It is not easy to obtain such high-quality dairy goods anymore. But, if you can find them, perhaps on a small farm, way out in the countryside, you'll find them worth the special search. Take my grandmother's word on it.

Crème fraîche: Method One

The first time I ate *crème fraîche* was in France, where I was served a bowl of plump, sun-ripened strawberries and a smaller bowl of the thickened, soured cream. Although I have since learned to use and serve it in a variety of ways, the fruit-accompanying bowl is still my favorite. Both of the following recipes make a fine *crème fraîche* with little discernible difference in taste.

1 cup heavy cream
3 teaspoons buttermilk

Combine the cream and buttermilk in a jar. Cover it tightly, and shake the mixture until thoroughly blended—about 1 minute. Set the jar on a shelf at room temperature, away from cold drafts. It needs to stand at least 8 hours at a temperature neither too hot or cold or it will not ferment properly.

When the *crème fraîche* is thick, store it in the refrigerator.

Makes a little more than 1 cup.

Crème fraîche: Method Two

Crème fraîche may be popular in France, but nowhere does soured cream enjoy greater affection than in Eastern Europe, where the invading Tartars influenced local cuisines with their clabbered-cream dishes.

1 cup sour cream
1 cup heavy cream

Whisk the sour cream in a bowl to thin it a bit. Whisk in the heavy cream until thoroughly combined. Cover the bowl with a tea towel and set it on a warm shelf. Let it stand until thick and sour—12 to 16 hours. When it is very thick, store it in the refrigerator.

Makes 2 cups.

Cassis Cream

What better way to breakfast in the summertime than with a bowl of sliced, ripe peaches smothered in *Cassis* Cream.

> *1 tablespoon red or black currant jelly*
> *¾ cup heavy cream*
> *½ teaspoon* crème de cassis *liqueur*
> *2 teaspoons dried currants (optional)*

In a small saucepan over medium-high heat, melt the jelly, and mash it with a fork to smooth it as it melts. When it is thoroughly melted, remove it from the heat. Set it aside to cool.

Whip the cream into stiff peaks. Fold in the cooled, melted jelly and the liqueur. If desired, for texture, stir in a couple of teaspoons of dried currants.

Makes a little more than 1 cup.

Crème pêche

I never run out of ways to eat peaches and raspberries. I probably love them more than does my boisterous cat, Sheldon B. Wabbit, who can consume as much of this addictive cream as I can. But then he weighs a slim 16 pounds and needs to keep up his strength. Serve *crème pêche* over fresh-picked raspberries.

> 1 cup heavy cream
> 2 teaspoons "runny" honey
> ⅛ teaspoon vanilla extract
> Pinch ground ginger
> ½ cup pureed, peeled, ripe peaches or
>   nectarines

Combine the cream, honey, vanilla, and ginger in a medium-sized mixing bowl. Using an electric or manual mixer, whip the cream until stiff peaks form. Add the peach puree a tablespoonful at a time, beating well after each addition.

Makes about 2⅓ cups.

English Lemon Curd

Serve on a toasted English muffin, as a filling for tartlets, or warm or chilled over fresh blueberries.

1 cup sugar
½ cup plus 2½ tablespoons
   unsalted butter
½ cup fresh lemon juice

3 whole eggs, beaten
3 egg yolks, beaten
1½ teaspoons minced lemon
   zest

Combine all ingredients in the top of a double boiler over simmering water. Whisk continually while the butter melts and the mixture thickens enough to coat a spoon. Take care it does not boil.

Use the lemon curd immediately over fresh blueberries; refrigerate it for other uses.

Keeps two weeks.

Makes 2½ cups.

Custard Cream Sauce with Cognac

This is the classic *crème anglaise*, that custardy, sweet sauce spooned over everything from fresh fruit and plain cakes to elegant, intricate desserts. Many recipes call for gelatin. This one doesn't.

3 egg yolks	1/4 teaspoon vanilla extract
2 tablespoons sugar	1 teaspoon cognac (or liqueur,
3/4 cup whole milk	if you prefer, such as
1/4 cup heavy cream	Grand Marnier)

Beat the yolks and sugar together in a large bowl. When they are thick and frothy, set them aside.

In a small saucepan, heat the milk, cream, and vanilla to boiling point. Remove from heat.

Using a hand-held electric mixer or a whisk, slowly beat a thin stream of the hot liquid into the egg mixture. Do not add the liquid too fast or add too much at a time, or the eggs will cook and lump.

Return the egg-and-milk mixture to the saucepan. Cook it over low heat, stirring continuously, until the mixture thickens into a custard. Do not let it boil. If tiny lumps appear, the heat is too high and the eggs are about to scramble—immediately remove the custard from the heat and whisk hard. If you proceed slowly, keep the heat low, and continuously stir, the sauce will come out perfectly—smooth and silky.

When the custard appears thickened and amply coats the back of a spoon, remove it from the heat. Transfer it to another container to cool it, maintaining the consistency.

Serve the sauce warm or chilled (but not reheated—it would curdle). If it will not be served until later, keep it refrigerated.

Makes about 1 cup.

Simple Yogurt

Simple Yogurt is indeed simple—and foolproof, providing you have the proper equipment. If you don't have an inexpensive candy thermometer (one that registers low temperatures) and a wide-mouth thermos, acquire them now. They will serve you for years.

Fresh, tart yogurt can be used as a base for uncooked sauces or as a substitute for such more caloric dairy products as sour cream or whole cream. It also makes a delicious breakfast when sprinkled with a few whole grains, nuts, and dried fruits. Or simply top fresh fruit slices with a dollop.

1 quart whole or low-fat milk
1 tablespoon unflavored yogurt

Using a candy thermometer in a medium-sized saucepan over medium-high heat, heat the milk to 180° to 185°F—no higher. Immediately remove the saucepan from the heat. Let the milk cool to 115° to 120°F—no lower. Stir in the fresh yogurt. Avoid the temptation to add more; it only makes the yogurt runny and sometimes prevents the souring process. Transfer the solution to a 1-quart wide-mouth thermos. Cap it tightly.

Let the mixture sit in a warm spot, undisturbed, for 4 to 8 hours. If you prefer a sweeter yogurt, check it after 4 hours. For extra firmness and tartness, let it sit a while longer. When it has the tartness you wish and appears somewhat solid, pour it into a clean jar and refrigerate.

Remember to save 1 tablespoon of your jar of yogurt as the starter for your next batch.

Makes 1 quart.

Yogurt Cheese

Yogurt cheese substitutes nicely for fatty cream cheese. In fact, I like it better for its tarter, more defined taste.

> *1 quart fresh, unflavored yogurt (see p. 141)*
> *½ teaspoon salt*
> *3 teaspoons mixed dried herbs, ground*

Line a colander with several layers of cheesecloth. In a bowl, combine the yogurt with the salt and ground herbs. Pour the yogurt mixture into the colander. Bring up each corner of the cheesecloth and tie them securely. Hang the cheesecloth bag over the sink or over a bowl to catch the dripping whey. Let the bag hang until all the whey has stopped dripping—18 to 24 hours.

Remove the cheese from the cheesecloth and wrap it tightly in plastic. Keeps one week in the refrigerator.

Makes about 2 cups.

Two-Mustard Cream with Green Onions

Excellent with poached chicken, fish, or grilled frogs' legs.

½ cup heavy cream
¼ cup sour cream
1½ tablespoons minced green onion

2 teaspoons coarse mustard
2 teaspoons green peppercorn mustard
½ teaspoon herb vinegar

In a small saucepan, bring the heavy cream to a boil over medium heat. Reduce the heat and simmer the cream until it reduces by half—to ¼ cup. Remove it from the heat, and cool.

Transfer the cooled cream to a small bowl. With a whisk, smooth out any lumps. Whisk in the remaining ingredients, one at a time.

Use immediately. (The sauce takes on a cooked egg yolk flavor after chilling.)

Makes about ½ cup.

Beurre manié

Beurre manié, while not a condiment, is a common ingredient in many recipes. You can make it up every now and then and store it in the freezer, for whenever a recipe calls for flour and butter or a roux. Keep one or two in the refrigerator—these instant thickener balls sure come in handy when a last-minute sauce fails to take the form expected.

Some people like to mix fresh or dried herbs into their *beurre manié*. I don't; the herbs in the current batch may not suit the recipe you plan to use. You could make several batches, each with different herbs, seeds, or seasonings. Just make sure you label the containers, as once the balls freeze it is difficult to tell which balls contain what herb.

½ cup unsalted butter, softened
8 tablespoons all-purpose flour

Using a fork, cream the butter and flour in a medium-sized bowl. When it is smooth and without lumps, roll the mixture into eight balls. If the mixture is too soft to roll, refrigerate it for 10 to 15 minutes.

Stack the balls in an air-tight container or plastic bag. Store them in the freezer until you're ready to transfer them to the refrigerator.

Makes 8 balls.

Maple Orange Butter

Perfect for waffles and hotcakes and scones and bran muffins and cornbread hot from the oven and . . .

½ cup unsalted butter, softened
3 tablespoons maple syrup
2 teaspoons packed orange zest
1 teaspoon orange juice

Place the softened butter in a small bowl. Using an electric or manual mixer, whip it until light and airy. Continue to whip, and add the syrup, then the orange zest and juice. Whip until they are thoroughly incorporated. Press the butter into a small decorative ramekin.

Serve the butter immediately or cover and refrigerate it until ready to use, but be sure to bring it to room temperature before serving.

Makes a little more than ½ cup.

Curry and Mango Butter

Place pats of this butter on top of chicken breasts before broiling.

½ cup unsalted butter, softened
1 tablespoon pureed ripe mango
1 teaspoon homemade Curry Powder (see p. 214)

Place all ingredients in a medium-sized bowl. Using an electric or manual mixer, whip the ingredients until thoroughly combined.

Roll the butter into a log in waxed paper to use by the slice. Keep refrigerated.

Makes about ½ cup.

Chervil Butter with Toasted Hazelnuts

Chervil contributes a delightfully refreshing flavor to this herbaceous spring butter. If you can't locate chervil, substitute parsley. Use pats of this butter to top fish fillets a minute before you are done grilling them.

> ½ cup unsalted butter, softened
> ⅓ cup toasted hazelnuts
> ¼ cup tightly packed fresh chervil leaves
> ½ teaspoon tightly packed, chopped fresh baby dill weed

Place all ingredients in a food processor. Pulse just until the nuts appear the size of small seeds.

Roll the butter into a log in waxed paper to use by the slice. Keep refrigerated.

Makes about ⅔ cup.

Green Butter

Years ago, few Americans had heard of arugula and sorrel, much less used them in the kitchen. Now, these slightly bitter lettuces can be found in many produce markets. They're marvelous in salads, pestos, and all sorts of sauces, as fillings for savory pastries, and in butters. This one is great over steamed vegetables, boiled potatoes, or tossed with freshly cooked pasta.

½ cup unsalted butter,
softened
¼ cup tightly packed fresh
arugula leaves
¼ cup tightly packed fresh
sorrel leaves

¼ cup tightly packed fresh
celery leaves
1 tablespoon chopped fresh leek
(white part only)
1 teaspoon chopped lemon zest

Put all ingredients in a food processor. Pulse until the butter appears creamy and bright green and the herbs are minutely chopped.

Press the butter into a small ramekin or mold, or roll it into a log in waxed paper to use by the slice. Keep refrigerated.

Makes ⅔ cup.

Mushroom Shallot Butter

Use for sautéeing fish or chicken, or softened as a spread for whole grain breads.

1 tablespoon unsalted butter
2 large mushrooms, sliced
1 medium shallot, peeled and sliced
½ cup unsalted butter, softened
1 garlic clove, pushed through a press

In a medium-sized skillet, melt the tablespoon of butter over medium-high heat. Add the sliced mushrooms and shallot. Sauté them until they are softened and the shallot appears translucent. Remove them from the heat; cool completely.

Place the mushroom mixture, the ½ cup of softened butter, and the garlic in a food processor. Pulse until the mushrooms and shallot become finely chopped.

Refrigerate the butter for a few minutes in a small bowl. When it is a bit firm, roll it into a log and wrap in waxed paper. To use, cut off slices.

Keep refrigerated.

Makes about ⅔ cup.

South of the Border Butter

Spread on warm tortillas or such soft seafood as grilled monkfish or lobster, or use to top freshly steamed vegetables.

½ cup unsalted butter, softened

2 tablespoons minced fresh cilantro (also called fresh coriander)

1½ teaspoons minced grapefruit zest

1½ teaspoons minced lime zest

1 teaspoon minced fresh jalapeño chile pepper (about ½ pepper)

1 teaspoon fresh lime juice

1 teaspoon fresh grapefruit juice

Combine all ingredients in a medium-sized bowl. Using an electric or manual mixer, whip them until creamy.

Press the butter into a small ramekin or mold, or roll it into a log in waxed paper and use it by the slice. Keep refrigerated.

Makes about ½ cup.

Smoked Salmon and Baby Dill
Butter with Capers

This butter is so divine you can easily eat it straight. If you must eat it on something, pair it with a very fresh, lightly toasted pumpernickel bagel. Open a bottle of champagne to wash them down, and enjoy!

½ cup unsalted butter, softened
3 ounces smoked salmon, chopped
2 tablespoons minced, fresh baby dill weed
2 teaspoons drained capers
1 teaspoon heavy cream

Place all ingredients in a medium-sized bowl. Beat with an electric mixer until the butter achieves a rosy salmon color and little flecks of dill appear throughout.

Press the butter into ramekins or small molds, or roll it into a log in waxed paper to use by the slice. Keep refrigerated. Bring to room temperature before serving.

Makes about ¾ cup.

Beurre fraise

A slightly sweet butter for topping waffles, hotcakes, or unsweetened baked goods.

½ cup unsalted butter, softened
3 large strawberries
1 tablespoon raspberry jam
1 teaspoon fraise *(strawberry) or* framboise *(raspberry) liqueur*

In a food processor, process all ingredients until the butter achieves a lovely, soft pink color. You may have to stop the machine periodically and stir down the sides.

Spoon the butter into heart-shaped molds and refrigerate. Just before serving, dip the outsides of the molds into tepid water and invert the butter onto small plates.

Makes almost ⅔ cup.

Chapter Six

THE SWEET TOUCH: PRESERVES, SYRUPS, FRUIT BUTTERS, AND DESSERT SAUCES

The first thing I remember tasting and then wanting to taste again is the grayish-pink fuzz my grandmother skimmed from a spitting kettle of strawberry jam. I suppose I was about four.

M. F. K. Fisher
The Art of Eating

Ever since honey was discovered, eons ago, people have been making all sorts of sweet sauces, preserves, and syrups. One of the earliest methods on record of preserving blackberries can be found in *De Re Coquinaira*, the early Roman cookbook by Apicius. Even earlier, lotus blossoms were reputed to have been made into a jam by the ancient Egyptians, who served it with roasted locusts. The affection for sweetened condiments has spanned centuries.

In the 1800s, jam making underwent tremendous improvements. Since the advent of the mason jar, scientifically based preserving methods, and strict attention to hygiene, jam making has become nearly foolproof. Before embarking on any of the canning recipes in this chapter, first read A Word About Canning, the appendix of this book. If you have canned but not made preserves before, you may wish to keep the following points in mind.

- Fruits and vegetables should be firm—slightly underripe—unless otherwise noted.
- Purchase fruits and vegetables at the height of their growing season for maximum flavor and minimum costs.
- When chopping produce, remember that pieces do not have to be perfectly uniform. Some roughness adds texture to the product, giving it a homemade quality.
- Do not reduce the amounts of sugar, honey, or corn or maple syrup given in the recipes. A reduction in sweetener can cause a preserve to jell improperly. Also, specific sweetening levels are required for proper food preservation. Too little sweetener could invite botulism.
- You can make up your own jam recipes by pairing 3 cups of sugar with every quart of prepared (peeled, pitted, and chopped) fruit. Add 6 to 8 citrus seeds, peels, or pits (or all three) tied in cheesecloth for pectin, and follow the directions of a similar recipe.

- Until you get a knack for ascertaining jell point, try using one of these time-tested methods.
    1. Use a candy thermometer. When it reads 221°F, the jam is ready.
    2. Stir a large metal spoon through the hot mixture. In the beginning, lots of little droplets will run off the back side. As the mixture approaches the jell point, the droplets will run thicker and separate into two drops, or streets of droplets. You have reached the jell point when the two drops appear to be running together into what is called a "sheet."
    3. If you think you have reached the jell point, but you're not sure, spoon a little of the mixture onto a small plate. Place the plate in the freezer for 2 minutes, then check the jam. If it appears thick and runs just a little, it's done. Be careful not to overcook the mixture (so that it becomes gooey); remember, it will firm up after it leaves the processing bath. If it does get overcooked, you can always return it to the pot, add some fruit juice to thin it out, bring it back to 221°F, and recan.
- After you process your jams, turn the jars upside down on a clean cloth. You will see the fruit float to the top. Turn the jar right side up again after 20 minutes. As the jar cools, the fruit will evenly distribute throughout the jar. Remember to store jars in a cool, dark, and dry spot.

Dried Fig Jam

Dried figs, when reconstituted, develop a deep, concentrated flavor.
The cardamom adds a sultry, exotic taste.

*2 (14-ounce) packages dried
    figs
5 cups water
⅓ cup fresh lemon juice*

*3 cups sugar
All seeds from juiced lemons
1 teaspoon ground cardamom*

Place the figs in a 4-quart pot. Cover with the 5 cups of water; partially cover the pot, and bring to a boil. Remove from heat and let stand, covered, for 1 hour, to plump the figs.

Remove the figs with a slotted spoon; reserve the cloudy water in the pot. Using kitchen shears, snip off the stems. Dice the figs by hand or in a food processor, and set them aside.

Add the lemon juice and sugar to the fig water. Cover it and bring it to a boil. Reduce the heat, and simmer 5 minutes. Stir in the chopped figs. Tie the seeds in several layers of cheesecloth, and add them to the mixture. Bring the mixture to a second boil, reduce the heat, and simmer just until slightly thickened—15 to 20 minutes. Remove from heat. Take out the tied seeds, and stir in the cardamom.

Ladle the jam into four sterilized, still-hot pint jars. Wipe rims, and cap immediately with still-hot lids, plus rings. Process 15 minutes in a boiling water bath.

Makes about 4 pints.

Red Pepper Preserves

Tanya Berry of Port Royal, Kentucky, doesn't remember where she got this recipe. She just knows she has been making it for an awfully long time. If you can get the vibrantly golden bell peppers now available in many markets, Mrs. Berry suggests using them as an alternative. Either pepper makes a spectacular sweet and slightly tart condiment. She also recommends using a food mill, but a food processor will amply substitute.

> *4 pounds red bell peppers, seeded*
> *2 tablespoons salt*
> *3 cups white distilled vinegar*
> *4 cups sugar*

The day before you make the preserves, dice the peppers by hand, in a food mill, or with the medium disk of a food processor. Add salt, and drain the peppers in a colander overnight.

The next day, press all the liquid out of the peppers; transfer them to a 3-quart pot. Stir in the vinegar and sugar. Over high heat, bring the mixture to a boil; reduce the heat to medium-high, and cook, uncovered, until thickened—about 45 minutes. Stir frequently to prevent sticking.

If you want to seal the preserves for shelf storage, ladle them into three sterilized, still-hot pint jars. Wipe rims, cap immediately with still-hot lids, plus rings, and process 10 minutes in a boiling water bath. Alternatively, store the preserves in the refrigerator for up to three weeks.

Makes 3 pints.

Blush of Summer Nectarine Preserves

These preserves are perhaps best appreciated on chilly January mornings when the vibrant orange-yellow color and rich, fruity flavor bring back memories of warm, balmy weather.

3 cups sugar
½ cup water
1 tablespoon fresh lemon juice
1 tablespoon fruit vinegar

4 cups (about 2 pounds)
    semifirm nectarines,
    peeled, pitted (pits
    reserved), and diced
1 cinnamon stick
¼ teaspoon vegetable oil
1 teaspoon minced lemon zest

Combine the sugar, water, lemon juice, and fruit vinegar in a 3-quart pot. Bring them to a boil over high heat. Add the diced fruit, remove the mixture from the heat, and let it stand for 1 hour.

Tie the cinnamon stick and nectarine pits in several layers of cheesecloth; add this to the pot. Stir in the oil and lemon zest. Bring the mixture back to a boil, over medium-high heat. Stirring occasionally, cook at a low boil until the syrup thickens and the fruit becomes translucent—about 30 minutes. Remove and discard the tied spice and pits.

Ladle the preserves into four sterilized, still-hot half-pint jars. Wipe rims and cap immediately with still-hot lids, plus rings. Process in a boiling water bath for 10 minutes.

Makes 4 cups.

Kiwi Preserves

I was eight years old the first time I laid eyes on a kiwi. Every day my family, new residents of Hawaii, saw, smelled, or tasted something new and unlike anything we had known on the mainland. The day my mother brought home a couple of fur-covered kiwis, I was certain they were small animals, or perhaps hairy eggs. At first, I was reticent to try them. After one bite of the bright green, sweet-and-sour center, I knew I would never be able to get enough—even in Hawaii they were almost prohibitively expensive. Today, due to an ample crop grown in California, they are no longer so costly or rare.

4 cups (about 2 pounds) kiwi fruit, peeled and diced
3 cups sugar
¼ cup fresh lemon juice
1 small strip lemon zest (about 2 inches long and ½ inch wide)
All seeds from juiced lemons

In a 3-quart pot, combine the fruit, sugar, and lemon juice. Tie the zest and seeds in several layers of cheesecloth; add this to the pot.

Bring the mixture to a boil over medium-high heat. Reduce the heat and simmer, stirring occasionally, until the preserves pass the "sheet test" (see the introduction to this chapter)—15 to 20 minutes. Discard the tied zest and seeds.

Ladle the preserves into four sterilized, still-hot half-pint jars. Wipe rims and cap immediately with still-hot lids, plus rings. Process in a boiling water bath for 10 minutes.

Makes 4 cups.

Eastern European Beet Preserves

Beets make a highly unusual jam. Either you are a beet aficionado or you are not; either you will adore this sweet and tart confiture or you will avoid it like the flu. Despite its controversial taste, I include it, because I wouldn't want someone who loves beets to miss it. Also, these are my grandmother's very favorite preserves. (You should see her eyes flash when I tell her I'm putting up a batch.)

3 pounds fresh beets, trimmed
5 cups white sugar
1 cup packed brown sugar
1 cup fresh lemon juice
⅓ cup chopped pecans

¼ cup minced candied ginger
(see p. 210)
2 teaspoons grated fresh
gingerroot
All seeds from juiced lemons

Bring a large pot of water to a boil. Place the trimmed beets in the boiling water; cook, covered, until the beets can be pierced through easily with a fork. Drain and cool them. Rub off the peels under cold running water. Chop the beets by hand or in a food processor.

Return the beets to the pot. Tie the lemon seeds in several layers of cheesecloth, and add this and all remaining ingredients to the pot. Bring the mixture to a boil over a medium-high flame. Reduce the heat to medium, and partially cover. Cook, stirring occasionally and skimming the froth, until the preserves begin to thicken—30 to 40 minutes. Discard the tied seeds.

Ladle the preserves into four sterilized, still-hot pint jars. Wipe rims and cap immediately with still-hot lids, plus rings. Process in a boiling water bath for 15 minutes.

Makes about 4 pints.

Quinces in Anise Syrup

No doubt about it, quinces make the prettiest of all fruit to preserve—bright, rose colored, and shimmering.

5¼ cups water
5½ cups sugar
3½ pounds quinces, peeled, cored, and chopped
1 tablespoon fresh lemon juice
½ teaspoon ground anise seed

In a large, 4- to 6-quart pot over high heat, bring the water and sugar to a boil. Add the quinces and lemon juice, and bring to a second boil. Reduce the heat and cook at a low, even boil, stirring occasionally. After 30 minutes, stir in the anise. When the mixture reaches a lovely rose color and the syrup thickens to corn syrup consistency—60 to 75 minutes—remove from heat.

Ladle the fruit and the syrup into nine sterilized, still-hot half-pint jars. Wipe rims and cap immediately with still-hot lids, plus rings. Process 10 minutes in a boiling water bath.

Makes 9 cups.

Sour Plum Conserve

This recipe makes a small quantity because sour plums are not generally available, though a few markets do carry them. If you can find the plums in abundance (such as on a neighbor's tree), double or triple the recipe. Just be sure to increase the cooking time accordingly, by 10 minutes per added pound of fruit.

1½ to 2 pounds small, ripe
    sour plums, peeled
1½ cups sugar
½ cup golden raisins
¼ cup dark raisins

¼ cup chopped pecans
¼ cup pine nuts
2 tablespoons fresh lemon juice
½ teaspoon vanilla extract

After peeling the plums (peels usually slip off readily), use a knife to scrape the pulp and juice into a measuring cup. You will need 2 cups of pulp and juice; the poundage will vary according to the ripeness and juiciness of the fruit.

In a 1½-quart saucepan over high heat, bring the plum pulp and the remaining ingredients to a boil. Reduce the heat to medium-high, and cook the mixture, stirring frequently to prevent sticking, until slightly thickened—15 to 20 minutes.

Ladle the conserve into three sterilized, still-hot half-pint jars. Wipe rims and cap immediately with still-hot lids, plus rings. Process 10 minutes in a boiling water bath.

Makes 3 cups.

Cherry Conserve with Grand Marnier

One of my very favorite fruits, made into a sinfully sweet condiment. The addition of liqueur adds to both its decadence and its allure.

2½ pounds firm cherries, pitted
½ cup raisins
4¾ cups sugar
¼ cup fresh lemon juice

2 tablespoons chopped pecans
2 tablespoons Grand Marnier or Cointreau
1 tablespoon minced orange zest

Combine the pitted cherries, raisins, and sugar in a 4-quart pot over medium heat. Simmer just until the sugar turns to syrup. Add the lemon juice, and bring the mixture to a boil. Stir in the pecans, liqueur, and orange zest. Reduce the heat to medium or medium-high, and simmer the mixture until it thickens—35 to 45 minutes.

As the conserve cooks, a great deal of froth will rise to the top; this must be discarded. Skim it with a broad spoon as it rises. So as not to lose fruit, nuts, and zest, skim the froth into a small strainer set over a cup. Press on the froth mixture a little as it drains; pour any fruit, nuts, or zest reserved in the strainer back into the conserve pot. You will need to do this several times during the course of cooking.

When the conserve reaches the jell point (as described in the introduction to this chapter), remove it from the heat and quickly ladle it into six sterilized, still-hot half-pint jars. Wipe rims and cap immediately with still-hot lids, plus rings. Process 10 minutes in a boiling water bath.

Makes 6 cups.

Cantaloupe Conserve

Most people don't readily associate fleshy cantaloupe or other melons with preserves. But they work just as well as other fruits. In fact, they make a more intriguing product, because your taste buds don't expect a melony flavor in a condiment.

6 cups diced ripe cantaloupe pulp (about 4 pounds whole melons)	*½ cup fresh or frozen pineapple juice*
2 cups diced, peeled papaya (about 2 pounds whole papaya)	*⅓ cup fresh lemon juice*
	6 cups sugar
	1 teaspoon minced lemon zest
	½ cup sliced almonds

Combine the diced cantaloupe, papaya, and pineapple juice in a 4-quart pot. Bring the mixture to a slow boil over high heat. Cover, reduce heat, and simmer 10 minutes. Stir in the lemon juice and sugar. Uncover, and again bring the mixture to a slow boil. Stirring occasionally, cook until slightly thickened—15 to 20 minutes.

Add the minced zest and sliced almonds. Continue cooking at a slow, even boil for 15 more minutes. The fruit should appear translucent and pass the "sheet test" (see the introduction to this chapter).

Ladle the conserve into seven sterilized still-hot half-pint jars. Wipe rims and cap immediately with still-hot lids, plus rings. Process 10 minutes in a boiling water bath. Remove the jars from the water, and wait for the pop from each lid that signals it has sealed. On a clean cloth, turn the jars upside down so the fruit distributes evenly as jars cool. Turn the jars right side up again.

Makes 7 cups.

Clementine Orange Marmalade with Ginger

Small Clementines, grown in the Middle East and Spain, are quite sweet, with a flavor very different from that of California or Florida oranges. Though available only in winter in a few produce markets, they will prove worth a search. Whether you eat them fresh or preserved as marmalade, they make the simplest meal a memorable one.

2½ pounds Clementine oranges
Juice and seeds of 1 lemon
5 cups sugar
¼ teaspoon ground ginger
1 tablespoon minced candied ginger

The day before you make the marmalade, peel the oranges and place the peel in a 3- to 4-quart pot. Cover the peels with water, bring them to a boil over high heat, then reduce the heat and simmer for 10 minutes. Drain the peels. Return the peels to the pot and cover them with fresh, cold water. Cover and let stand overnight.

Seed the oranges, reserving the seeds for later use. Puree the orange sections in a food processor or blender. Press the juice through a fine sieve, and discard the pulp. There should be approximately 2 cups of juice. Cover and refrigerate overnight.

The next day, drain the orange peels and rinse them under cold running water. Drain them and transfer them to a food processor. Pulse just until the peels are roughly chopped. Return the chopped peels to the pot. Tie the lemon seeds and orange seeds in several layers of cheesecloth and add them to the pot with the reserved orange juice and the lemon juice and sugar.

Over high heat, bring the mixture to a boil. Reduce heat. Simmer, skimming the froth, until the mixture is slightly thickened—30 to 45 minutes. Stir in the gingers. Discard the tied seeds.

Ladle the marmalade into five sterilized, still-hot half-pint jars. Wipe rims and cap immediately with still-hot lids, plus rings. Process 10 minutes in a boiling water bath.

Makes 5 cups.

Tangerine Marmalade

How pretty tangerines look hanging on boughs of deep green leaves. Their deep orange color makes a magnificent marmalade, blissfully sweet and slightly sour. Like other citrus marmalades, this preserve will jell in the jar; be sure not to overcook it.

> 2½ pounds tangerines
> Juice of ¼ pound lemons, seeds reserved
> 5 cups sugar
> ¼ teaspoon vegetable oil

The day before you make the marmalade, juice the tangerines and reserve the seeds. Store the juice and seeds, separately, in the refrigerator. Scrape the pulp from the tangerines and discard it. Place the peels in a 4-quart pot, cover them with water, and bring them to a boil. Boil the peels for 5 minutes. Drain the peels and cover them with fresh water; let stand overnight.

The next day, drain the peels again, to remove all bitterness. Using a spoon, scrape out the remaining white pith from the peels and discard it. Dice the peels by hand or in a food processor. Return the peel to the 4-quart pot and add the reserved tangerine juice and lemon juice, sugar, and oil. Tie the reserved tangerine and lemon seeds in several layers of cheesecloth and add this, too, to the pot.

Over high heat, bring the mixture to a boil. Reduce heat and partially cover. Stirring occasionally, simmer the mixture until thickened and syrupy—40 to 45 minutes. When it reaches the thickness of maple syrup, remove it from the heat and skim any froth. Discard the tied seeds.

Ladle the marmalade into five still-hot half-pint jars. Wipe rims and cap immediately with still-hot lids, plus rings. Process 10 minutes in a boiling water bath. This marmalade is more liquid than most and should be turned upside down while cooling, to distribute the peel, more often than most—every 15 minutes until completely cool.

Makes 5 cups.

Kumquat and Grapefruit Marmalade

Save this recipe for a blustery winter weekend. It's time consuming but makes a glorious marmalade, redolent of a warm, beachside citrus grove.

> 2½ pounds grapefruit
> 1½ pounds kumquats
> Juice of 1 lemon, seeds reserved
> 10 cups sugar

With a sharp knife, carefully remove the yellow zest from the grapefruits. Place the zest in a large bowl.

Cut the grapefruits in half. Using a curved knife, cut the sections of pulp and the juice out of the membranes. Place the pulp and juice in a second bowl. Reserve the seeds. Squeeze the remaining juice into the bowl.

Halve the kumquats lengthwise. Remove and reserve the seeds. Use a grapefruit spoon to scoop the kumquat pulp into the bowl with the grapefruit pulp and juice. Add the kumquat peels to the bowl with the grapefruit zest. Cover and refrigerate the fruit pulp and juice overnight.

Transfer the peels to a large pot, cover them with water, and bring them to a boil over high heat. Boil 5 minutes. Remove the pot from the heat and let it cool. Drain the peels, and cover them with fresh water; again drain, and cover them with fresh water. Cover the peels and let them stand overnight.

The next day, drain the peels thoroughly and chop them coarsely, by hand or in a food processor. Return the chopped peel to the large pot.

In a food processor or blender, puree the fruit pulp and juices. Add the puree to the chopped peel in the pot. Stir in the sugar. Tie all the reserved seeds in several layers of cheesecloth, and add this and the lemon juice to the pot.

Over medium-high heat, bring the mixture to a simmer. Cook it until it thickens—25 to 35 minutes. Discard the tied seeds. This marmalade is easy to overcook; make sure it is still runny when spooned onto a plate (see the tests for reaching jell point in the introduction to this chapter). Bear in mind it will firm up both as it cools and while stored.

Ladle the marmalade into nine sterilized, still-hot half-pint jars. Wipe rims and cap immediately with still-hot lids, plus rings. Process 10 minutes in a boiling water bath.

Makes 9 cups.

Carrot with Date Marmalade

Carrots may seem like an odd ingredient for a jam. Yet carrots make marvelous cakes, breads, puddings, and other sweet delicacies; why not jam?

5 cups (about 1 pound) shredded carrots
¼ pound oranges
¼ pound lemons

All seeds and hulls of juiced oranges and lemons
4 cups sugar
½ teaspoon vanilla extract
½ cup chopped dates

Place the shredded carrots in a 3-quart pot.

Using a peeler or zester, remove the zest layer of the citrus fruits; mince it and add it to the shredded carrots. Squeeze the juice of the fruit into the pot, reserving the seeds. Tie the seeds and citrus fruit hulls into several layers of cheesecloth; add this, also, to the pot. Stir in the remaining ingredients.

Bring the mixture to a boil over medium-high heat. Reduce the heat. Simmer the mixture, stirring frequently, until it passes the "sheet test" (see the introduction to this chapter)—about 30 minutes. Discard the tied seeds and hulls.

Ladle the jam into four sterilized, still-hot half-pint jars. Wipe rims and cap immediately with still-hot lids, plus rings. Process in a boiling water bath for 10 minutes.

Makes 4 cups.

Pumpkin Confiture

A confiture is nothing more than a jam, or, in this case, a marmalade. I like to serve Pumpkin Confiture as a topping for pound cake. It adds flavor and mystique to an otherwise plain dessert.

*5 pounds fresh, whole
    pumpkin*
½ pound lemons, seeded
½ pound oranges, seeded

1 cup fresh orange juice
10 cups sugar
1 vanilla bean

After washing the pumpkin, remove the stem and peel. Cut the pumpkin into quarters; scoop out all the threads and seeds. Using the grating disk on a food processor, grate the pumpkin quarters, lemons, and oranges, retaining all juices. (You can grate the fruit by hand, but it takes much longer.)

Transfer the grated mixture and the additional cup of orange juice to a 5-quart pot. Stir in the sugar and vanilla bean, completely mixing the sugar and juice.

Over high heat, bring the mixture to a boil. Reduce the heat, partially cover, and simmer the mixture until it is thickened and the pumpkin begins to appear translucent—40 to 60 minutes. Because this jam is easy to overcook, you may wish to use a candy thermometer (in which case, cook to 220°F, no higher) or apply one of the other jell tests explained in the introduction to this chapter. The confiture should be quite liquid, like a thick sauce. It finishes jelling later.

Remove the vanilla bean and ladle the confiture into (depending on how much you cook it down) six or seven sterilized pint jars. Wipe rims, cap immediately with still-hot lids, plus rings, and process 10 minutes in a boiling water bath.

Makes 6 to 7 pints.

True Blueberry Syrup

While blueberry syrup goes marvelously with rich, custardy ice creams and thick puddings, I like it best simply mixed with carbonated water over ice to quench an unrelenting thirst.

1½ pounds blueberries
3 cups water
1 tablespoon minced lemon zest
3 cups sugar (approximately)
1 nutmeg, split in half (tap carefully with a hammer)

Combine the berries, water, and zest in a 4-quart pot over medium-high heat. Crush the berries with a potato masher as they soften. Bring the mixture to a boil; stir once or twice while it boils hard for 2 minutes. Remove from heat.

Set a large bowl in the sink. Place a cheesecloth-lined colander inside the bowl. Pour the berry mixture into the colander and tie the ends of the cheesecloth around the faucet. Let the juice drip from the berry bag until the dripping stops—a few hours. Save the juiced berries for another use.

Measure the berry liquid; return it to the pot and, for each cup, add ¾ cup sugar. Add the split nutmeg. Over medium-high heat, bring the mixture to a boil. Reduce the heat and simmer the mixture until it is reduced by one-third—about 20 minutes. If you want it extra thick and sweet you can reduce it by as much as half.

Let the syrup cool. Pour it into a clean quart jar and refrigerate. Keeps several weeks refrigerated.

Makes about 1 quart.

Lime Syrup

Unless you have a lime tree or access to one, making quantities of lime syrup can be a costly venture. So this recipe uses only three to four pieces of fruit, well within economic reason. If you do have a tree, feel free to double or triple the amounts given. Also, for a change, you might wish to substitute other citrus fruits, such as lemons, grapefruits, or tangerines. Use any of these syrups to dress fruit compotes, as a base for spritzer drinks, or as a poaching liquid for fruit.

1 cup sugar
½ cup fresh lime juice
½ cup water
½ teaspoon minced lime zest

Combine all the ingredients in a medium-sized saucepan, over medium-high heat. Bring the mixture to a boil. Let it cook at a slow boil until it is reduced by one-fourth, about 10 minutes. Strain the syrup and let it cool.

Pour the syrup into a clean jar and refrigerate.

Makes about 1¼ cups.

Champagne Currant Syrup

In a pinch, this recipe can be executed with seedless red or black grapes. I like to use it to dress mixed fruit compotes. If cooked down to a thicker state than is described here, it can be spooned over tarts, ice cream, or pound cake.

>*1 pound stemmed fresh currants*
>*1 cup sugar*
>*½ cup champagne*
>*1 teaspoon fresh lemon juice*
>*Pinch ground cardamom*

Thoroughly puree the currants in a food processor or blender. Pour the puree through a fine sieve into a medium-sized saucepan. Press firmly on the solids with the back of a broad spoon to release all the juices. Discard the solids.

Add all the remaining ingredients to the currant juice. Over medium-high heat, bring the mixture to a boil. Stir occasionally while the mixture boils, until it is reduced by half. Remove the syrup from the heat and let it cool. Pour the syrup into a clean jar and re-frigerate it.

Makes about 2 cups.

Minted Vanilla Syrup

I often keep a selection of syrups in the refrigerator for spur-of-the-moment ideas. Besides using this simple syrup in spritzer drinks, fruit compotes, and poaching liquid for pears, a spoonful gives a cup of hot or iced coffee an extra kick.

2 cups sugar
2 cups water
1 cup coarsely chopped mint leaves
¼ teaspoon vanilla extract

Combine all ingredients in a medium-sized saucepan. Over high heat, bring the mixture to a boil. Stir it, reduce the heat, and cook it at a slow boil for 10 minutes. Remove it from the heat and let it cool to room temperature.

Pour the syrup through a sieve into a clean jar and refrigerate it.

Makes about 2¾ cups.

Honey, Peach, and Brandy Butter

The summer I finished writing this book, my husband and I moved into an old house with a huge backyard full of orchard trees. All of a sudden I had more peaches, cherries, apples, apricots, and figs than I knew what to do with. I was just finishing this chapter when the boughs on the small peach tree began to bend so low from the weight of ripe fruit that they nearly broke. This recipe represents the end result of my effort to rescue the little tree. And yes, the tree made it. Now if I can just find a way to use the thousands of wild blackberries overgrowing the north end.

5 to 5½ pounds almost-ripe peaches, peeled, pitted (pits reserved), and chopped	1¾ cups sugar
	¾ cup honey
	¼ cup peach brandy or unflavored brandy
1 cup water	

Place the chopped peaches in a 4-quart pot with the water. Cover, bring the mixture to a simmer, and cook until quite soft—15 to 20 minutes.

Using a slotted spoon, transfer the peaches to a food processor or blender. Reserve the cooking liquid in the pot. Puree the peaches until smooth and measure them; you should have 5 cups of puree. If not, prepare a few more peaches in the above manner. (Puree yields vary according to the fruit's ripeness.)

Combine the puree with the cooking liquid in the pot. Stir in the sugar, honey, and brandy. Tie the peach pits in several layers of cheesecloth and add this to the mixture. Partially cover. Turn up the heat to medium and simmer, stirring frequently to prevent sticking, until the butter is quite thick—about 45 minutes.

Ladle the butter into six sterilized, still-hot half-pint jars. Wipe rims, cap immediately with still-hot lids, plus rings, and process in a boiling water bath for 10 minutes.

Makes 6 cups.

Early American Pumpkin Butter

This recipe makes a lot of butter, and for good reason; it serves as the perfect gift during the holiday season. The traditional spicing and hint of maple sweetness will enhance old-fashioned holiday meals.

6 cups cooked pumpkin puree (see below)	1 teaspoon ground cinnamon
	1 teaspoon ground nutmeg
2 cups pure maple syrup	½ teaspoon ground ginger
2 cups light corn syrup	¼ teaspoon ground cloves
2 cups packed brown sugar	¼ teaspoon ground mace
2 teaspoons fresh lemon juice	¼ teaspoon vanilla extract

Put the puree in a 4-quart pot; stir in the maple syrup and corn syrup. When these are thoroughly combined, add the remaining ingredients. Set the pot over medium-high heat. When it begins to boil, partially cover it; the mixture will splash profusely. Cook the puree at a slow boil, stirring frequently to prevent sticking, until it thickens and turns a darker color—about 45 minutes.

Ladle the butter into five sterilized, still-hot pint jars. Wipe rims and cap immediately with still-hot lids, plus rings. Process for 25 minutes in a boiling water bath.

TO MAKE PUMPKIN PUREE

Either bake the fruit or boil it. To bake pumpkins, put them in the oven whole, on a cookie sheet, at 350°F until softened and collapsed. (Be sure to poke holes in them first, or they will explode in the oven.) Scoop the pulp away from the peel. Puree the pulp in a blender or food processor. Or, boil peeled chunks of fresh pumpkin until softened. Then puree the cooked pulp. If you don't want to bother making your own puree, you can use two 29-ounce cans of commercial pureed pumpkin.

Makes 5 pints.

Double Apricot Butter

Most fruit butters are essentially just that—fruit. This one also contains chopped dried fruit and walnuts, ingredients that add a little more body and a lot more character. If you prefer your butter smooth and creamy, omit the dried fruit and nuts. Just remember in that case to sterilize fewer jars, since the recipe will make considerably less.

2¼ pounds ripe apricots, peeled, halved, and pitted
2 cups sugar
¼ cup orange juice
1 cup chopped walnuts
½ cup chopped dried apricots

In a food processor or blender, finely puree the apricot halves. Transfer the puree to a 3-quart pot and add the remaining ingredients. Partially cover, turn up heat to medium or medium-high, and simmer the mixture until thick—20 to 25 minutes. Be sure to stir the bottom and sides of the pot frequently to prevent sticking and burning. If the puree seems to be cooking too fast, turn the heat down. When the butter is done, use a shallow spoon to remove the froth from the surface.

Ladle the butter into four sterilized, still-hot half-pint jars. Wipe rims and cap immediately with still-hot lids, plus rings. Process in a boiling water bath for 10 minutes.

Makes 4 cups.

Pear Butter

Use any kind of pear for this recipe, but keep the type consistent; mixing varieties obscures minute flavor differences.

*3½ pounds pears, peeled,
   cored, and chopped
3 tablespoons cider vinegar
3 tablespoons water
2 cups sugar
⅓ cup fresh orange juice*

*½ teaspoon ground allspice
¼ teaspoon ground nutmeg
⅛ teaspoon ground mace
⅛ teaspoon ground cloves
1 vanilla bean*

Combine the pears with the cider vinegar and water in a 4-quart pot. Bring the mixture to a boil over high heat. Cover and reduce heat. Simmer the mixture, stirring occasionally, until the pears soften—25 to 30 minutes.

With a slotted spoon, transfer the pears to a blender or food processor; puree them until smooth. Stir the puree into the poaching liquid that remains in the pot. Add the sugar, orange juice, spices, and vanilla bean. Stir the mixture until well blended.

Partially cover the pear mixture and set it over medium heat. Stir frequently to prevent the mixture from sticking, while you cook it until very thick—45 to 60 minutes. Remove the vanilla bean.

Ladle the butter into four sterilized, still-hot half-pint jars. Wipe rims and cap immediately with still-hot lids, plus rings. Process in a boiling water bath for 10 minutes.

Makes 4 cups.

Quince Cheese

Fruit "cheeses" enjoy great popularity in the British Isles. They are similar to butters, except that they have a thicker consistency—they can be sliced with a knife—and require more sugar. Also, preparation tends to be more time consuming, but every scrumptious bite is worth it. Try quince cheese with breakfast muffins.

> *10 cups peeled, cored, and chopped quince (5 to 6*
> *quinces)*
> *5 cups sugar*
> *½ teaspoon ground spice such as anise, cardamom,*
> *cinnamon, ginger, or nutmeg*

In a 4-quart pot, cover the quince with water and a lid. Bring to a boil over high heat. Reduce the heat and simmer the mixture until the quince becomes very tender—1 to 1½ hours, depending on the size of the pieces.

Drain the quince, puree it thoroughly in a food processor or blender, and return it to the pot. Stir in the sugar and the desired spice. Cook the mixture over medium-low heat, partially covered. Stir frequently to prevent sticking. When the mixture reaches fruit butter consistency—in 30 to 45 minutes—uncover it and begin stirring continually to prevent possible burning. The mixture will actively bubble and burp. Stir and cook in this manner until it is quite thick—another 30 to 45 minutes. You will know it has reached the cheese stage when, as you pull a spoon through it, you can clearly see the pot's bottom and the mixture only slowly flows back into place.

To prepare the cheese for shelf storage, ladle it into five sterilized, still-hot half-pint jars. Wipe rims and cap immediately with still-hot lids, plus rings. Process 10 minutes in a boiling water bath. Or, if desired, spoon the cheese into an oiled, 2½-pint mold. When it is cool, cover it with plastic or foil, and refrigerate it overnight. To serve the cheese, invert the mold onto a plate.

VARIATIONS

You can substitute pears, apples, or a combination of both, for quince.

Makes 5 cups.

Fresh Strawberry Sauce

Nothing quite compares to red, ripe strawberries bursting with summer sweetness. They make a luscious sauce. Use over ice cream or waffles, as a filling for trifle or cakes, to top pudding, or to blend with pureed bananas and yogurt for a high-energy breakfast drink.

1 pound fresh strawberries, trimmed and halved
½ cup sugar
2 teaspoons fresh lemon juice

⅛ teaspoon vanilla extract
1 tablespoon fraise *(strawberry),* framboise *(raspberry), or* crème de cassis *(black currant)* liqueur

In a large saucepan, combine the strawberries, sugar, and lemon juice. Mash the berries with the back of a fork to release their juice, and bring the mixture to a boil over medium-high heat. Reduce the heat to medium. Continue to mash the berries as necessary, and simmer until they are soft through—15 to 20 minutes.

Transfer the berries and liquid to a blender or food processor. Puree them until smooth. Add the liqueur; pulse once or twice to barely incorporate it.

Cool the sauce to room temperature and refrigerate it. Keeps several days in the refrigerator.

Makes 1 pint.

Kiss of Honey Berry Sauce

Almost any summer berry will work for this recipe. I prefer to use olallieberries or other blackberries, boysenberries, raspberries, or tayberries. Serve over rich, custardy ice cream, in trifle, over fresh fruit, or as a topping for light puddings.

> *2 cups freshly picked berries*
> *¼ cup honey*
> *1 tablespoon fresh lemon juice*

Combine the berries with the honey and juice in a small saucepan. Over medium-high heat, bring the mixture to a boil. Reduce the heat slightly and simmer the mixture, stirring occasionally, for 5 minutes.

Transfer the mixture to a food processor or blender. Pulse until no whole berries appear. Pour the mixture through a fine sieve set over a bowl; stir with a broad spoon until only seeds remain in the strainer. Discard them.

Either use the sauce immediately or refrigerate it for use within a few hours. Keeps for several days.

Makes 1¼ cups.

Chunky Applesauce

My brother, Joey, has always loved applesauce the way others adore chocolate. As a youngster, he ate as many as three bowlfuls at one sitting. Now, a little older, but no less passionate about the quality of his applesauce, he only eats a bowl or two at a time.

5 pounds firm, tart green
apples, peeled, cored, and
diced
Juice of 2 lemons
½ cup water

1⅓ cups sugar
⅛ teaspoon ground nutmeg
⅛ teaspoon ground ginger
⅛ teaspoon ground cinnamon

As you prepare the apples, toss them with the fresh lemon juice to prevent them from turning brown. Transfer the apples and juice to a 4-quart pot. Over medium-high heat, bring them to a slow boil; reduce the heat to medium and simmer the mixture, covered, until the apples soften—about 10 minutes.

Using a potato masher, mash the apples in the pot. Do not try to mash them perfectly; some should be chunky. Stir in the sugar and spices and cook 5 more minutes.

Ladle the hot applesauce into four still-hot, sterilized pint jars. Wipe rims and cap tightly with still-hot lids, plus rings, and process 20 minutes in a boiling water bath.

Makes 4 pints.

Caramel Sauce with a Dash of Rum

According to my sister and my editor, both of whom profess to be caramel fanatics, only one proper type of caramel sauce exists: the gooey, thick mixture that sticks mercilessly to the roof of your mouth. I tend to like mine a little less adhesive. If you like yours like Jordana's and Kate's, cook it for an extra 5 minutes at the end.

> *1½ cups sugar*
> *½ cup water*
> *½ cup heavy cream*
> *1 tablespoon rum*

Put the sugar in a heavy, medium-sized saucepan. Over medium-high heat, cook it for 10 minutes, stirring occasionally, until the sugar melts into an amber, smooth syrup. Remove the saucepan from the heat. Pour in the water, and stir vigorously until the furious bubbling subsides. Mix in the cream and rum. Reduce the heat to medium and cook the caramel until thickened—5 more minutes.

Serve this sauce warm.

Makes 1¾ cups.

Mandarin Chocolate Cream Frosting

How a recipe for frosting got in here I'm not sure. But take note of it for your next cake, as a filling for a layered torte, or as a little sweet something in which to dip fresh-baked madeleines.

½ cup unsalted butter,
    softened
1½ cups confectioners' sugar
2 ounces unsweetened
    chocolate, melted and
    cooled

1 teaspoon orange zest, grated
    (optional)
⅛ teaspoon salt
1 tablespoon fresh orange juice
1 tablespoon Cointreau

In a medium-sized bowl, cream the butter and 1 cup of the confectioners' sugar with an electric mixer. Beat in the melted chocolate, orange zest, and salt. When the mixture is fluffy, add the remaining sugar alternately with the orange juice and Cointreau.

Use this frosting immediately.

Makes about 1½ cups.

Gingered Papaya Curd

This is not a curd in the traditional sense, because it requires neither eggs nor cooking. Nevertheless it looks and can be used very much like the thickened, lusciously sweet mixtures we spoon into tartlets or over fresh fruit, or simply spread on warm toast.

1½ cups peeled, seeded, and cubed fresh papaya (about 1 medium)
2 tablespoons sugar
1 tablespoon fresh lemon juice
2 teaspoons minced gingerroot

Place all ingredients in a food processor or blender. Process until pureed but still thick.

Use the curd immediately, or refrigerate it until ready to serve.

Makes ¾ cup.

Chapter Seven

A PINCH OF THIS, A DASH OF THAT:
MISCELLANEOUS TREASURES

There is another class of foods, called condiments,
which should not pass unnoticed.

Mary Lincoln
The Boston Cookbook (1894)

Not long after my parents married, my father, who was raised on traditional Russian Jewish cooking, began asking my mother to make such things as blintzes, kugel, matzobrie, and borscht. My mother, who was an excellent cook, knew nothing about this cuisine. So she thought, "I'll ask Buba to teach me." Buba, my paternal grandmother, agreed.

Mama went to Buba's house early on a Friday morning to watch Buba make that night's Sabbath dinner, a weekly ritual during which the family came together and Buba ruled as matriarch.

Mama entered the kitchen to find Buba busily making matzo balls.

"Where's your cookbook?" Mama asked.

"No cookbook," Buba responded with her thick, Eastern European accent.

"How do you know how much of everything to put in?"

"I know," Buba smiled, "I've been making dem long time, since I was vely little. My modder taught me dese recipes and her modder taught her." Buba delved into a cabinet, searching.

Mama stood shyly by, watching Buba's every move. After a while she asked, "What is that flour?"

"Not flour," my grandmother responded, "eetz matzo meal."

"Well, how much do you use?"

"Oh, some," Buba answered noncommittally.

Mama knitted her brow. "How much is some?"

"I don't know. Maybe a handfool."

Mama looked at Buba's hands. They were small, much smaller than her own. What kind of recipe was this? As the day progressed, her confusion grew. Everything came in dashes, pinches, handfuls, and somes. But Mama was determined. As she watched Buba cook, she took scrupulous notes, estimating the dashes and pinches. She went home and practiced her rudimentary recipes until my father confirmed she had them right. Today, we're still using Buba's recipes. Except that now they are easier to follow.

Buba's dashes and pinches were much like the recipes in this chapter—a little of this, a little of that. While Buba's dashes fit into a place—a recipe—the products in this chapter do not fit into a category or, for that matter, into any of the other chapters. Hence, they compose a miscellaneous chapter of their own. Here you will find such delights as Drunken Fruit, Tomanade, Cajun Spices, and a horseradish to warm your soul, if not, in fact, your bloodstream.

Tomanade with Basil and Capers

Toss this with hot pasta, spread it on baguette slices, or use it to stuff baby eggplants or artichoke hearts or to fill button mushrooms.

⅔ cup pitted Kalamata or Niçoise olives

7 oil-packed sun-dried tomato halves (see p. 204)

1½ cups loosely packed fresh basil leaves

1½ teaspoons drained capers

1 large garlic clove, pushed through a press

2 tablespoons virgin olive oil

1 teaspoon berry vinegar

Place the olives, tomatoes, basil, capers, and garlic in a food processor or blender. Pulse until all these ingredients are chopped. With the machine running, slowly add the olive oil and vinegar. Stop and stir down the sides frequently. It should not be a smooth puree, but a textured paste.

Serve the tomanade immediately or refrigerate it. If you do refrigerate it, be sure to let it sit at room temperature for a couple of hours before serving.

Makes about ¾ cup.

Anchovy Paste

For a fast and easy hors d'oeuvre, spread a little anchovy paste sparingly on fresh slices of French bread. Top each with a *cornichon* cut lengthwise into a fan shape.

2 (2-ounce) cans anchovies, rinsed and patted dry
1 to 4 garlic cloves, minced (according to taste)

4 tablespoons toasted coarse French bread crumbs
4 teaspoons virgin olive oil
1 ½ teaspoons fresh lemon juice
2 ½ teaspoons drained capers

Using a mini-size processor or a mortar and pestle, blend all the ingredients until a smooth paste is achieved.

Keeps several weeks in the refrigerator.

Makes about ¾ cup.

Candied Orange Peel

Bakers often use candied citrus peels to decorate cakes, tortes, and cookies. They add texture and color to the tops of such smooth desserts as cheesecake.

>3 oranges
>¾ cup sugar
>⅓ cup water
>2½ tablespoons orange juice
>2 cups additional sugar (approximately)

With a small knife, remove the orange part of the peel. On a chopping board, slice the removed peel into long, thin strips. Set them aside.

Cook the sugar, water, and orange juice in a small saucepan over medium heat. When the liquid reaches a boil, stir in the orange peel. Cook it until it is quite soft and translucent—10 minutes.

With a slotted spoon, transfer the peel to a large bowl. Pour in the additional sugar, tossing the peel until it is thoroughly covered in crystals. With your fingers, pick one piece at a time out of the sugar and lay it on a cookie sheet. Let the pieces dry for 48 hours.

Store the candied peel in an airtight container in a cool spot.

VARIATIONS

Lemon peel or tangerine peel can be substituted for the orange peel.

Makes 1 to 1½ cups, depending on the size of the oranges.

Frosted Fruit

At holiday time, frosted fruit surrounding a roast turkey, pork crown roast, leg of lamb, or game creates a beautiful effect. Frosted fruit not only looks spectacular but guests also love to eat these sweetened tidbits.

Fresh blueberries, cherries, cranberries, grapes, or currants or a
combination, in clusters or stemmed
½ cup water
¾ cup sugar
1 cup additional sugar (approximately)

After washing the fruit, towel it as dry as you can. Spread it on a fresh towel to air dry thoroughly.

While the fruit continues to dry, combine the water and the ¾ cup sugar in a small saucepan. Bring it to a boil. Let the syrup cool completely. It should be slightly thick.

Pour the additional sugar on a large piece of waxed paper. Dip the fruit by the cluster or spoonful into the sugar syrup. Roll the pieces immediately in sugar. When no more sugar will stick, set the fruit to dry on another piece of waxed paper.

Vanilla Sugar

Use this in place of regular sugar. It's particularly nice in hot tea.

1 to 2 cups sugar
1 vanilla bean, split open lengthwise
1 stick dried cinnamon, broken in half
1 nutmeg, split in half (tap carefully with a hammer)

In your sugar bowl or another small, covered container of sugar, bury the vanilla bean. If you would like a little spice as well, add the cinnamon and nutmeg.

Leave the sugar for at least a week. Check it after seven days; when it is flavored enough, remove the bean and spices.

ABOUT REUSE

Don't throw away your vanilla bean; you can use it again. Simply wash it off, dry it thoroughly, and store it in a jar or plastic bag.

Makes 1 to 2 cups.

Sun-Dried Tomatoes
Packed in Olive Oil

Chop and toss into pasta salads or green salads, top steamed vegetables or sautéed eggplant, or use in recipes, such as Tomanade (p. 199).

Ripe plum or Roma tomatoes, peeled (see Notes to the Cook)
Salt
Fresh or dried chiles
Garlic cloves, halved
Extra-virgin olive oil

Halve each tomato lengthwise, core it, and use a teaspoon to remove the seeds and juice. After thus preparing the entire batch, dust the tomatoes with salt and toss them to distribute it.

Lay the tomatoes on mesh screens. Prop the screens on bricks or stilts on a table outside in the sun. Cover this with another screen. Air should be able to circulate freely, but the screens should prevent bugs and debris from entering.

Leave the tomatoes to dry all day in the sun, each day for several days. In the evening, when the temperature goes down, bring the tomatoes and screens inside. In the middle of the summer, in areas where the temperature gets into the nineties or hundreds, drying will take only a couple of days. If the temperature is cooler, drying may take up to a week. Check the tomatoes each day, and turn them over periodically. When they are dry and almost rubbery, take them out of the sun.

Pack the dried tomatoes in hot, clean jars. Add to each a dried or fresh chile, if you would like them a little spicy, and a halved garlic clove. Cover with extra-virgin olive oil. Cap the jars and store them in a cool, dry spot.

ALTERNATIVE DRYING METHOD

Another way to dry tomatoes is to bake them in the oven. It's much less energy efficient, but quicker—and if you don't have a place outdoors to execute the recipe, it's the only alternative.

Prepare the tomatoes as described above. Arrange them on liberally oiled wire racks set over cookie sheets. Bake the tomatoes at 150°F for 5 to 6 hours. Check them after 3 hours; they may need rearrangement on the racks if the oven has hot spots. After 5 hours of baking, turn the tomatoes over. Bake them another 5 hours. Small tomatoes should have become dry and leathery; larger or thicker tomatoes may require another 30 to 60 minutes of baking. Pack the tomatoes in jars according to the directions above.

Layered Drunken Fruit

Layered Drunken Fruit can be made with one or many fruits and any type of colorless liquor you prefer. Experiment according to your personal taste. Serve alongside cakes and baked puddings or in a compote dish to complement butter cookies.

Cherries
Slightly underripe apricots
Peaches
Plums
Nectarines
Grapes
Firm raspberries

Blackberries
Blueberries
Cranberries
Clear or white liquor or
*   liqueur such as rum, gin,*
*   vodka, or anisette*

In a sterilized wide-mouth quart jar, pack any combination of the fruits listed. (Avoid citrus fruits and fruits that turn brown, such as bananas.) Slice the larger fruits. Layer slices and berries by color. Cover each layer with the liquor or liqueur; use the same kind for the entire jar. After each addition, cap the jar tightly.

Once the entire jar has been filled, let it sit undisturbed for three days before serving. It will keep three months, but bear in mind that the fruit gets stronger (or "drunker") each day. At three months, a few good bites may make you tipsy.

Makes 1 quart.

Fried Herbs

Fried herbs make a savory and slightly crunchy addition to a meal. Use them to garnish whole fish, chops, or roast game or lamb.

Several sprigs of fresh herbs, stems and leaves intact
¼ cup flour
¼ teaspoon salt
Dash cayenne pepper
Vegetable oil

Wash and thoroughly dry the herbs. In a small bowl, combine the flour, salt, and cayenne pepper. Dust the herbs thoroughly with the flour mixture.

Heat 1 inch of oil in a small skillet until it fries a pinch of flour; maintain this heat, which is about medium-high. Fry the herbs in the hot oil just until crisp—45 to 60 seconds. The herbs should not lose their shape or brown more than lightly. Remove the herbs with a slotted spoon, and drain them on a plate lined with absorbent toweling.

Makes enough to garnish one platter.

Bagna cauda

The first time I heard a French friend discuss *bagna cauda*, I thought it sounded terribly cosmopolitan, even romantic . . . two people huddled over a bowl of a hot liquid fragrant with truffles, garlic, and anchovies . . . the crusty hunks of chewy peasant bread each dips, then washes down with robust, crimson wine from the Italian countryside . . . the couple content to share this simple meal in a rustic little restaurant. The English name, *hot bath*, doesn't quite conjure up the same blissful images. Nevertheless, the taste remains the same—sensual.

1 cup unsalted butter	*2 fresh truffles or morels,*
4 tablespoons olive oil	*thinly sliced*
4 garlic cloves, pushed through	*4 cups fresh vegetables, cut*
a press	*into bite-size pieces; or 4*
7 anchovy fillets	*cups French bread, cubed*
	and toasted

Combine the butter and oil over medium-low heat in a shallow skillet. Skim the froth as it rises. When the butter has melted, cook the garlic in the skillet for 3 minutes. Take care not to let it brown. Remove the mixture from the heat, and stir in the anchovies.

Set the skillet over low heat. Continue to stir and cook the mixture until the anchovies become a paste. (You may need to continue skimming froth.)

Remove the *bagna cauda* from the heat. Stir in the sliced truffles or morels. Pour it into a shallow bowl and serve immediately with vegetables or toasted French bread. If you have a small warming plate for use at the table, use it under the *bagna cauda*.

Serves 4 as a first course; 8 as an hors d'oeuvre.

Fresh and Feisty Horseradish

The food processor was surely invented for this pungent little condiment. You can execute the recipe with a hand grater, but I assure you the fumes will overwhelm your breathing tract. Besides that, the horseradish comes out creamier in a processor. This recipe makes a large quantity; it lasts forever in the refrigerator. Horseradish can be used in sauces and for other uses, but I like it best with gefilte fish or roast beef.

> *1 pound horseradish root, peeled and coarsely chopped*
> *1 cup white distilled vinegar*
> *2 tablespoons white wine vinegar*
> *1 teaspoon salt*

Process the horseradish pieces in a food processor until the root appears shredded. Slowly add the vinegars and salt. Continue processing for another 1 to 2 minutes; stop when the horseradish takes on a creamy consistency.

Spoon the horseradish into a quart jar or large plastic container. Keep it refrigerated for a week before use; the horseradish will age slightly and flavors will heighten.

Makes 1 quart.

Tapenade

[ITALIAN OLIVE PASTE]

Tapenade sets the perfect mood for dinners laden with garlic; guests get enticed with a taste of what is to come. Use tapenade to fill cherry tomatoes, marinated baby eggplant halves, or artichoke hearts. Or simply serve it with thick slices of crusty peasant bread. Refrigerate if not using within 2 to 3 hours. Bring back to room temperature before serving.

8 ounces Niçoise olives
2 ounces green olives without
    pimentos
1 (6-ounce) can California
    black olives, drained well
1 (2-ounce) can anchovies,
    drained
3 garlic cloves
2 large fresh morels (optional)
¼ cup virgin olive oil
2 tablespoons capers, drained

Pit the olives; squeeze the skin of each olive with your fingers until the pit pops through. Rinse the anchovies thoroughly in a strainer under cool running water (to reduce their saltiness), and pat them dry with absorbent toweling.

Combine the olives, anchovies, garlic, and morels in the bowl of a food processor. With the machine running, slowly add the oil. When the ingredients appear pastelike, cease processing. Spoon the tapenade into a bowl, and stir in the capers.

Makes about 2 cups.

Harissa

[MOROCCAN HOT SAUCE]

Many North African dishes call for this fiery paste mixture. Although you can buy it commercially, it's just as simple to make at home. I first learned to make this sauce many years ago from a Moroccan woman living on a farm near the coastal town of Ashkelon, in Israel. She used it in much greater quantities than I did—but then, my tolerance for searing hot food was not as great as hers.

There are several ways to make this sauce. For example, Paula Wolfert, surely this country's grandest expert on Moroccan cooking, also uses caraway seeds and occasionally a roasted pimento.

For a quick and piquant dressing to serve with raw vegetables or grilled chicken, or as a dipping sauce for meats, add a small amount of *Harissa* to ½ cup of mayonnaise and 2 to 3 tablespoons of Dijon mustard.

¼ cup dried chile flakes
2 tablespoons ground cumin seed
2 garlic cloves, pushed through a press
3 tablespoons virgin olive oil
Pinch salt

Mix all the ingredients in a small bowl. Transfer to a jar, and store in the refrigerator. *Harissa* keeps several months.

Makes about ⅓ cup.

Candied Ginger

No doubt about it, candying ginger takes hours and patience. The investment is well repaid, however. Commercial candied ginger costs a pretty penny; depending on the cost of ingredients in your area, a batch of homemade can cost as little as a couple of dollars. Use it to decorate cakes, pastries, or cookies; as an ingredient in preserves; or simply for snacking when you crave a little sweet.

1 ½ pounds firm gingerroot
2 ½ cups sugar
1 vanilla bean
1 tablespoon fresh lemon juice
3 cups sugar (approximately)

Peel the gingerroot and slice it in ⅛-inch- to ¼-inch-thick rounds. Don't discard the little "knees." Peel and dice them as best you can.

Bring 2 quarts of water to a boil in a 2 ½- or 3-quart pot. Add the ginger, cover, reduce the heat to medium, and cook the ginger until the pieces soften—1 ¼ to 1 ½ hours.

Set a colander in a large bowl or over a very large measuring cup in a sink. Pour in the ginger and cooking liquid. Reserve the ginger. Measure out 2 cups of the liquid, and return it to the pan with the sugar, vanilla bean, and lemon juice. (Discard the remaining liquid.) Bring the mixture to a boil over high heat. Stir in the drained ginger. Turn down the heat, cover, and simmer the syrup until reduced to about 1 cup. This should take about 1 ½ hours. Drain the ginger and cool it completely. The syrup may be reserved for another use, such as poaching apples. Wash and dry the vanilla bean for future use.

Roll two to three pieces of cooled ginger at a time in a bowl of the sugar. Set the candied ginger on racks or cookie sheets to dry for 24 hours; if it is still sticky and moist, it probably was not cool enough when you rolled it. Simply toss it in the sugar again and leave it to dry once more.

When the ginger is no longer sticky but feels fairly dry, store it in airtight jars in a cool spot. In warm weather areas, ginger may have to be kept refrigerated.

Makes 5 cups.

Quatre épices

Used often in pâtés and on vegetables. French recipes for many other kinds of dishes call for it as well. As with other spice mixtures, grind the whole spices fresh for best results.

> *1 tablespoon freshly ground nutmeg*
> *1 tablespoon ground ginger*
> *1 tablespoon freshly ground cloves*
> *2 teaspoons ground white pepper*

Mix the ingredients and store them in a small jar on a cool, dark, dry shelf. Since the spices go stale quickly, this recipe makes only a small amount.

VARIATIONS

The four spices above are those traditionally found in *quatre épices* mixtures. If you wish, you may add or substitute cinnamon, allspice, a little mace, or cardamom.

Makes about ¼ cup.

Pickling Spices

Pickling spices can consist of any spice that suits your taste. You may wish to put together your own combination. I particularly like this one for its subtle lacing of coriander seeds.

6 small dried red chile pods,
    crumbled
2 tablespoons crumbled bay
    leaves
¼ cup mustard seed

¼ cup dill seed
¼ cup coriander seed
1 tablespoon celery seed
1 tablespoon white peppercorns

Mix all the ingredients and store them in an airtight jar on a cool, dark, dry shelf. The spices go stale quickly; make up only as much as you will use in a month.

Makes 1 cup.

Curry Powder

Curry powders often are blended of twenty or more spices. Historians believe they were first made in the ancient city of Mohenjo-daro in what is now Pakistan. This area is credited with inventing the mortar and pestle, a device used to crush whole spices into powders. Whether you use a mortar and pestle or a small grinder, make the powder fresh from as many whole spices and seeds as possible, for maximum flavor and pungency.

1½ tablespoons ground
turmeric

3 tablespoons ground
coriander seed

2 teaspoons ground fenugreek
seed

1 teaspoon ground cumin seed

1 teaspoon ground cinnamon

1 teaspoon ground ginger

½ teaspoon ground dried chile
flakes

½ teaspoon ground black
peppercorns

½ teaspoon ground mustard
seed

¼ teaspoon ground mace

¼ teaspoon ground anise seed

¼ teaspoon ground bay leaves

Mix the ground spices and store them in a cool, dark, dry spot. As with other spices, once ground this mixture will keep its strength only a few weeks, so make only as much as you will use within a month's time.

Makes about ⅓ cup.

Garam Masala

Garam masala, a spice mixture fundamental to Indian cuisine, can be made quite easily at home. Freshly ground whole spices create the finest result. In fact, it is well worth purchasing a small coffee grinder just for this purpose. If you must substitute commercially ground spices, make sure they are the freshest available.

1 tablespoon ground cardamom

1 tablespoon ground cinnamon

2 tablespoons ground cumin seed

2 tablespoons ground coriander seed

1 teaspoon ground cloves

1 teaspoon ground black peppercorns

⅛ teaspoon ground white peppercorns

½ teaspoon ground nutmeg

In a small skillet, over medium heat, roast the ground spices separately. Combine them in a small jar and store the mixture in a dark, cool, dry spot.

Make only as much as you think you will use in a short period of time. *Garam masala*, as with all ground spices, will lose its potency within about a month of grinding.

Makes about ⅓ cup.

Cajun Spices

Whether you lean toward "Cajun" or "Creole," Louisiana-style cooking enjoys new-found popularity all around the nation. In recent years restaurants serving this exciting regional cuisine have opened in every major city, coast to coast. Despite European and African influences, Louisiana-style cooking is strictly American. You might call it a melting-pot cuisine or a fine example of what can happen when people from different nations and different traditions come together in a new land abundant with unusual produce, spices, seafood, and meats.

3 bay leaves, crushed or ground
½ teaspoon freshly ground black peppercorns
½ teaspoon ground white pepper
¼ to ½ teaspoon cayenne pepper (or more, if you like your food hot)
1 teaspoon salt

½ teaspoon dried thyme
¼ teaspoon dried or ground sage
1 teaspoon filé powder
¼ teaspoon dry mustard powder
½ teaspoon onion powder (if necessary)
½ teaspoon garlic powder (if necessary)

Mix all the ingredients. If the recipe for which you are preparing the spices does not call for fresh garlic and onions, include the onion and garlic powders.

Provides ample spicing for 1 jambalaya or gumbo recipe that feeds 4 to 6 people.

Bouquet garni

A key ingredient in stocks, soups, stews, sauces, and vegetable dishes.

5 fresh parsley stalks with leaves
1 sprig fresh thyme
1 stalk celery
1 large bay leaf

Either tie one parsley stalk around the herbs and celery or tie a small piece of string or several layers of cheesecloth around all of them. (If you plan to dry the herbs and store the *bouquet garni*, omit the celery.)

Use the fresh *bouquet garni* immediately, or store it, air dried, in an airtight container.

Makes a bouquet garni *for one dish.*

Fines herbes

Toss into salads, vegetable dishes, terrines, egg dishes, or cream or broth soups.

In summer, when herbs are fresh and abundant, make up batches of *fines herbes* for use all winter long. Herbs can be dried on screens in the summer sunlight, in very-low-temperature ovens, in microwave ovens, or simply on a paper towel in a sunny window. To keep the mix fresh longer, store the jars in the refrigerator.

> *3 tablespoons dried chervil*
> *2 tablespoons dried parsley*
> *1 tablespoon dried tarragon*
> *1 teaspoon dried chives*
> *1 teaspoon dried basil*

Mix the herbs and store them airtight in a cool, dark, dry spot or the refrigerator.

Makes about ⅓ cup.

Appendix

A WORD ABOUT CANNING

Preserve that old kettle, so blackened and worn,
It belonged to my father, before I was
born. . . .

Edward Harrigan
"My Dad's Dinner Pail"

The first time I put up preserves, I was terrified. I was afraid of doing something wrong, of giving a jar to someone and the person falling ill, or worse.

Wait a minute, I thought, this isn't the Dark Ages! Techniques have long been perfected. There must be a way to do it right, as well as wrong. Just do it right the first time, I told myself, and then you won't have to fuss and worry. So I read the directions and followed each step carefully, maybe even too carefully. To my surprise, the blackberry jam came out perfectly—dark, thick, and sweet as honey—the jars shimmered with deep purple color. I was most astounded by the ease. It wasn't half as difficult as I imagined. Then I felt rather foolish; I thought of all those years I could have been canning but hadn't, because I was intimidated by a little jar and its lid.

Since that day when I shed my preserving phobia, I have been canning happily. And, to satiate my curiosity, I've read volumes of material on canning practices. Indeed, a number of years ago there was every reason to fear a jar of home-canned goods. But not anymore. With the advent of the vacuum-pack lid, canning is just about foolproof. I say *just about* because no procedure or jar in the world will protect a poorly executed recipe or the wrong canning process, such as canning in a water bath instead of by pressure.

Let's get things straight from the beginning. What is pressure canning? Two types of food exist: acid and low acid. The former contains natural acid, an element that protects against bacteria growth. Acids have their own yeasts and molds, but they are easily destroyed, in the case of canning foods, by heating filled jars in a large pot of boiling water (a "boiling water bath"). The internal jar temperature climbs to 212°F and kills the microorganisms.

Low-acid foods, such as meats, poultry, seafoods, and certain vegetables, contain other kinds of bacteria, ones that cannot be destroyed at 212°F. They must be heated to 240°F in a pressure canner, a device like a pressure cooker.

In this book, we will be concerned only with one method—the boiling water bath—and with one type of food—acid. So, you don't have to run out and buy all sorts of fancy equipment. In fact, you probably already have most of what you will need.

- One large canning kettle or stockpot with a tight-fitting lid. It must be large enough for jars to be completely covered by 1 inch of water.
- One wire rack to fit into the bottom of the kettle, or a canning basket. The rack or basket keeps jars off the kettle bottom. The basket keeps jars away from the pot's sides and from each other, as well.
- One pair of tongs.
- One pair of jar lifters.
- One plastic funnel, preferably specially manufactured for canning.
- One heavy 4- to 5-quart pot for cooking.
- One medium-sized saucepan for heating jar lids.
- Spoons, ladles, and knives of various sizes.
- Cheesecloth, rags, and toweling.
- Timer.
- Jars with vacuum-pack lids: half-pints, pints, and quarts.
- A colander, a scale, and several different-sized strainers.

You're ready to can; what do you do first? Decide which jars to use. See your recipe for the jar size. Check the jar rims for cracks and chips. Discard any with even minor abrasions, or the lids won't fasten securely and hold the required vacuum. The metal rings may be reused, as long as they stay rust- and dent-free. Vacuum lids can only be used once. I always prepare one jar, lid, and ring more than I need, as a backup, just in case I've underestimated how much the recipe will make or, during jar filling, I discover a nick.

Wash the jars, lids, and rings in hot, soapy water. You can combine washing the jars with sterilizing them if instead you run them through a dishwasher (don't open the dishwasher door when the cycle finishes, as the jars need to stay hot until ready to use). I find it simpler, though, to wash them by hand, then fill the canning kettle with water, put the rack or basket in place, cover the kettle, and set it over high heat. When the water boils, immerse the washed jars (using jar lifters). Make sure the water completely covers the jars by at least 1 inch. Boil 5 minutes. Reduce the heat to low, and leave the kettle covered, until you're ready to fill the jars and process them.

After cleaning the lids and rings, place them in a saucepan of water; cover it, bring it to a boil, and boil it for 5 minutes. Then reduce the heat to low, and leave the lids and rings in the hot water until needed.

The more you can, the better you will be able to gauge your cooking time and preparation of equipment. If I am preparing a recipe with a long cooking time, 45 minutes or more, I will get my equipment ready while the mixture cooks. For a short cooking time, 30 minutes or less, I will get everything ready ahead. There's nothing worse than overcooking a beautiful preserve because you have to stop and get your jars ready. Even if you're packing cold vegetables in a jar (for pickling), keep the jars in warm water. Otherwise they may crack later when you put them in the water bath.

Now you've followed the recipe and you're ready to start filling. Using the jar lifters, take a sterilized jar out of the kettle or dishwasher. Carefully pour its contents back into the kettle. Place the jar upright on a clean cloth. Small amounts of water left on it will quickly evaporate. Pack cold vegetables by hand; place a funnel on top of the jar to pack liquids. Canning funnels have a line that shows how far up to fill the jar. If you aren't using one of these funnels, fill the jar to ⅛ inch to ¼ inch from the top. Take another jar out of the kettle, and place it on the cloth; remove the funnel from the first jar, place it on the second, and turn back to the first. If any air bubbles appear inside this filled jar, run a rubber spatula around the inside walls until they release. Using clean, wet absorbent toweling, wipe around the jar's top rim to remove any drops that may have spilled.

The smallest drop of anything but water can prevent a proper seal. Using tongs, remove one vacuum lid from the hot water and place it evenly on top of the jar. Use the tongs to remove a metal ring and screw it on securely. Set this prepared jar to the side while you fill the remaining jars the same way. In the meantime, turn up the heat under the kettle. The water should reach a rolling boil by the time you finish the filling.

When all the jars are filled, use jar lifters to place them in the boiling kettle. (If it isn't boiling yet, wait.) Be sure the water covers the jars by at least 1 inch. Cover the kettle. The rolling boil subsides when the jars enter the water; count the processing time from when it resumes. Process the jars for the time specified in the recipe. (Remember that pints require 5 minutes longer than half-pints.) For recipes in this book canned at 1,000 feet above sea level, add an extra minute of processing time for the first 20 minutes or 2 minutes for recipes requiring over 20 minutes in the hot water bath. Each additional 1,000 feet requires another minute for short processing and 2 minutes for longer times. To prevent overcooking, remove the jars promptly at the end of the processing time.

Take the jars out, one at a time, with lifters, placing them on a clean towel. Wipe off water from the tops. Some jars may already be vacuum sealed. You can tell by tapping on the lid: if it doesn't bounce or it stays down, it's sealed. Don't worry about those that bounce. Within a few minutes you should hear a popping sound—that's the lid pulling in and pushing the air out. Any jars that do not seal or stay down when you press on them should be refrigerated when cool. Those with secure seals can be stored when they have reached room temperature, in a cool, dark, dry spot.

If you're making a preserve, jam, or jelly, keep in mind that the contents take 12 to 24 hours to firm up. Immediately after processing they appear as juice. They will get nice and thick later.

Be sure the spot where you store your preserved gems is cool, dark, and dry. You may feel inclined to set them out in a light spot to show them off. (After all, you worked hard, why not let everyone see your efforts?) Unfortunately, light will fade the brilliant colors and leave your jars looking a little dull. Moisture and heat can lead to their demise as well. So tuck them away in a shady, dry pantry, and they will keep a very long time.

One last word of caution—nothing to fret over, just something to keep in mind. Spoilage occasionally occurs, even when it seems you followed all the rules and processed correctly. How can you recognize spoilage?

You take a jar out of the pantry and you notice:
· The contents seeping out of the jar.
· A broken seal.
· An unusual odor.
· Mold growing around the label.
· A bulging lid.
You open a jar and:
· Liquid spurts out.
· You smell gassy fumes.
· The contents appear slimy and cloudy.
· Mold covers the top.

If any of these conditions occurs, close the jar. Whatever you do, do not taste any of it or give it to an animal. Double wrap the jar in foil. Seal it with tape. Enclose it in a plastic bag so the smell can't be detected. Make it difficult for either human or animal to recognize it as food. Discard it in the trash.

And now you're disappointed. What went wrong? Are all the jars from that batch spoiled? Not necessarily. Many things contribute to spoilage.

Particles may have dropped on the jar rim during filling, preventing a good seal. This would be an isolated spoilage. Other jars, if the rims were cleaned, should be okay.

You might not have noticed a very tiny crack in the jar. This minute fracture may have caused an improper seal in only that jar.

Perhaps you altered the sugar, vinegar, or salt content in the recipe, or used homemade wine vinegar with a questionable percentage of acidity. Particularly in canning recipes, certain levels of sugar and salt and strengths of vinegar are required for proper preservation. Vinegars should have a minimum of 4 percent but preferably 5 percent acidity. If the amounts of the ingredients were changed, the contents may have spoiled because there wasn't enough natural preservative for the new proportions. In this case, if you found one bad jar, chances are the whole batch will be bad. Recipes should be followed as written.

Possibly you doubled or tripled a recipe and affected preservation capacities of key ingredients. Unless advised, do not increase a recipe.

And last, but unfortunately most important, you may have rushed and not read the instructions properly. Maybe you didn't wait until the water reached a rolling boil before you began to count the processing time, so the bacteria didn't get destroyed. Or maybe you forgot to process. If this could be what happened, all you can do is take it a little slower next time, read the directions carefully, and try again.

Good luck. I am sure that once you can one or two recipes you will find it quite rewarding. I have no doubt you will be pleased with both the results and yourself.

Index of Recipes by Title

Index of Recipes by Ingredients

Design by David Bullen
Typeset in Mergenthaler Galliard
by Wilsted & Taylor
Printed by Fairfield Graphics
on acid-free paper